The Psychology of Narcissism

Understanding Narcissistic Personality Disorder and its Impact on Relationships, Work, and Self-Identity

Lewis Finan

Table of Contents

Introduction

In an age where self-promotion is often celebrated and social media platforms amplify personal achievements, the term "narcissism" has become increasingly prevalent in everyday conversations. But what does it truly mean to be narcissistic? Beyond the casual usage lies a complex and multifaceted psychological condition known as Narcissistic Personality Disorder (NPD). Understanding this disorder is essential not only for those who might be affected by it but also for those who interact with individuals exhibiting narcissistic traits in their personal and professional lives.

"The Psychology of Narcissism: Understanding Narcissistic Personality Disorder and its Impact on Relationships, Work, and Self-Identity" delves into the intricate world of NPD, offering readers a comprehensive exploration of this pervasive and often misunderstood condition. Through a blend of clinical insights, real-life case studies, and the latest psychological research, this book aims to demystify narcissism and provide a deeper understanding of its implications.

Narcissism is more than just an inflated sense of self-importance or a craving for admiration. It encompasses a range of behaviors and thought patterns that significantly affect how individuals perceive themselves and relate to others. This book explores the origins of narcissistic traits, examining the interplay between genetic, environmental, and social factors. It also addresses the diverse manifestations of narcissism, from overt grandiosity to covert vulnerability.

One of the critical aspects of understanding NPD is recognizing its impact on relationships. Narcissists often have tumultuous interpersonal dynamics, marked by a lack of empathy, manipulative behaviors, and a constant need for validation. This book provides insights into how these traits affect romantic relationships, friendships, and family dynamics, offering practical advice for those navigating these challenging interactions.

In the workplace, narcissism can have both positive and negative consequences. While some narcissistic traits, such as confidence and ambition, can lead to professional success, they can also result in toxic work environments and strained colleague relationships. This book examines the dual-edged sword of narcissism in professional settings, providing strategies for managing and mitigating its adverse effects.

Self-identity is another crucial area impacted by narcissism. Individuals with NPD often experience fragile self-esteem, masked by a façade of superiority. This book delves into the psychological mechanisms behind this paradox, exploring how narcissists perceive themselves and how their self-identity evolves.

Whether you are a mental health professional seeking a deeper understanding of NPD, someone who suspects they might have narcissistic traits or an individual trying to navigate a relationship with a narcissist, this book offers valuable insights and practical guidance. By shedding light on the complexities of narcissism, "The Psychology of Narcissism" aims to foster empathy, promote healthy relationships, and encourage personal growth and self-awareness.

Join us on this enlightening journey into the depths of narcissism, as we uncover the psychological underpinnings of this disorder and its profound impact on various aspects of life. Through understanding comes the power to heal, transform, and build more meaningful connections with ourselves and others.

Chapter 1: Introduction to Narcissism

Narcissism—a term that has made its way from the clinical lexicon to everyday conversation—often evokes images of vanity, self-obsession, and a relentless quest for admiration. But what lies beneath the surface of this complex personality trait? In this first chapter, we embark on a journey to uncover the essence of narcissism, tracing its origins, defining its characteristics, and exploring its multifaceted nature.

What is Narcissism?

Narcissism originates from the Greek myth of Narcissus, a young man who fell in love with his reflection. This myth encapsulates the central theme of narcissism: an intense preoccupation with oneself. However, narcissism in psychological terms is far more nuanced than mere self-admiration. It encompasses a spectrum of behaviors and attitudes that influence how individuals interact with the world around them.

At its core, narcissism involves a pervasive pattern of grandiosity, a constant need for admiration, and a lack of empathy for others. These traits can manifest in various degrees, from healthy self-confidence to pathological self-centeredness. Understanding where narcissism falls on this spectrum is crucial for recognizing its impact on individuals and their relationships.

Historical Perspectives

The study of narcissism has evolved significantly over the past century. Early psychoanalytic theories by Sigmund Freud and his contemporaries laid the groundwork for understanding narcissism as a developmental stage and a defense mechanism. Freud described narcissism as an integral part of human development, where individuals first invest their libidinal energy in themselves before directing it towards others.

Over time, the concept of narcissism expanded beyond psychoanalysis. Researchers and clinicians began to identify different forms of narcissism, such as grandiose and vulnerable narcissism. Grandiose narcissists are characterized by overt arrogance, a sense of entitlement, and a desire for power and recognition. In contrast, vulnerable narcissists exhibit hypersensitivity, defensiveness, and fragile self-esteem masked by outward humility or introversion.

Narcissistic Personality Disorder (NPD)

When narcissistic traits become extreme and pervasive, they may constitute Narcissistic Personality Disorder (NPD). NPD is a clinically recognized mental health condition that significantly impacts an individual's thoughts, emotions, and behaviors. According to the Diagnostic and Statistical Manual of Mental Disorders (DSM-5), NPD is defined by a consistent pattern of grandiosity, a need for admiration, and a lack of empathy, beginning in early adulthood and present in various contexts.

Individuals with NPD often struggle with interpersonal relationships, as their need for validation and lack of empathy create conflicts and misunderstandings. They may exhibit manipulative behaviors, exploit others for personal gain, and react aggressively to perceived criticism. Understanding NPD requires delving into its diagnostic criteria, exploring its underlying psychological mechanisms, and recognizing its impact on daily life.

The Spectrum of Narcissism

Not all narcissism is pathological. Healthy narcissism, characterized by self-confidence, ambition, and resilience, can be beneficial in moderation. It enables individuals to pursue their goals, maintain self-respect, and navigate social interactions effectively. The challenge lies in distinguishing between healthy and unhealthy narcissism, as the line between them can be thin and context-dependent.

Narcissistic traits can fluctuate over time and across different situations. For instance, someone may exhibit narcissistic behaviors in high-stress environments or during significant life transitions. Recognizing these variations helps us understand the dynamic nature of narcissism and its potential triggers.

The Importance of Understanding Narcissism

Understanding narcissism is vital for several reasons. Firstly, it enhances our ability to recognize and address narcissistic behaviors in ourselves and others. By identifying the signs of unhealthy narcissism, we can take steps to foster healthier relationships and improve emotional well-being.

Secondly, understanding narcissism sheds light on its impact on various domains of life, including personal relationships, professional environments, and self-identity. This knowledge equips us with the tools to navigate complex interactions, manage conflicts, and support those affected by narcissistic behaviors.

Lastly, studying narcissism contributes to the broader field of psychology by deepening our understanding of personality disorders and human behavior. It challenges us to question our assumptions, refine our diagnostic criteria, and develop more effective therapeutic interventions.

In this introductory chapter, we have laid the foundation for a comprehensive exploration of narcissism. By defining narcissism, tracing its historical development, and distinguishing between healthy and pathological forms, we have set the stage for a deeper dive into this fascinating and often misunderstood aspect of human psychology.

As we progress through the subsequent chapters, we will delve into the origins of narcissism, its manifestations in relationships and work, and its impact on self-identity. Through this journey, we aim to unravel the complexities of narcissism, fostering greater empathy, awareness, and strategies for dealing with its challenges. Welcome to the intricate world of narcissism—a realm where self-love, self-loathing, and self-awareness intersect in profound and often surprising ways.

1.1 Definition and Overview of Narcissistic Personality Disorder (NPD)

Narcissistic Personality Disorder (NPD) is a complex psychological condition that falls under the category of personality disorders. It is characterized by a pervasive pattern of grandiosity, a constant need for admiration, and a lack of empathy for others. These traits begin in early adulthood and manifest in various contexts, significantly impacting an individual's interpersonal relationships, self-image, and behavior. To comprehend the full scope of NPD, it is essential to delve into its diagnostic criteria, underlying mechanisms, and its distinction from general narcissistic traits.

Diagnostic Criteria

The Diagnostic and Statistical Manual of Mental Disorders, Fifth Edition (DSM-5), provides specific criteria for diagnosing NPD. According to the DSM-5, an individual must exhibit five or more of the following traits:

- **Grandiosity**: An exaggerated sense of self-importance, often without commensurate achievements.
- **Preoccupation** with Fantasies: Persistent fantasies about unlimited success, power, brilliance, beauty, or ideal love.
- **Belief in Being Special and Unique**: A conviction that one is unique and can only be understood by, or should associate with, other special or high-status people.
- **Need for Excessive Admiration**: A constant need for excessive admiration and attention from others.
- **Sense of Entitlement**: Unreasonable expectations of especially favorable treatment or automatic compliance with one's expectations.
- **Interpersonally Exploitative**: Taking advantage of others to achieve one's ends.
- **Lack of Empathy**: An inability or unwillingness to recognize or identify with the feelings and needs of others.
- **Envy of Others**: Envying or believing that others are envious of oneself.
- **Arrogant Behaviors or Attitudes**: Displaying arrogant, haughty behaviors or attitudes.

These criteria highlight the pervasive and enduring nature of NPD, which goes beyond occasional narcissistic behaviors that many people might exhibit at times.

The Spectrum of Narcissism

It is important to understand that narcissism exists on a spectrum. Not everyone who exhibits narcissistic traits has NPD. The spectrum ranges from healthy narcissism, which involves self-confidence and ambition, to pathological narcissism, which significantly impairs an individual's ability to function in everyday life.

- **Healthy Narcissism**: Involves a realistic sense of self-esteem, confidence, and the ability to assert oneself. It is characterized by a positive self-image and the capacity to form healthy relationships.
- **Pathological Narcissism**: Involves excessive self-focus, a lack of empathy, and dysfunctional interpersonal relationships. This form of narcissism can lead to significant distress and impairment in various areas of life.

Understanding this spectrum helps differentiate between normal variations in self-esteem and the more severe, inflexible patterns seen in NPD.

Underlying Psychological Mechanisms

NPD is thought to arise from a combination of genetic, environmental, and psychological factors. Some of the key contributing factors include:

- **Early Childhood Experiences**: Adverse childhood experiences, such as neglect, abuse, or excessive pampering, can contribute to the development of narcissistic traits. Inconsistent or excessive validation can distort a child's self-perception and expectations from others.

- **Genetic Predisposition**: There is evidence to suggest that genetics may play a role in the development of NPD. Certain personality traits, such as high levels of extraversion and low levels of agreeableness, can be inherited and may predispose an individual to develop narcissistic tendencies.
- **Psychodynamic Factors**: Psychodynamic theories suggest that narcissism is a defense mechanism developed to protect fragile self-esteem. Individuals with NPD may create an inflated self-image to shield themselves from feelings of inadequacy and low self-worth.

Impact on Relationships

One of the most significant consequences of NPD is its impact on interpersonal relationships. Individuals with NPD often struggle to form and maintain healthy relationships due to their need for admiration, lack of empathy, and exploitative behaviors. They may:

- **Struggle with Intimacy**: Their inability to understand and connect with others emotionally can hinder the development of deep, meaningful relationships.
- **Exhibit Manipulative Behaviors**: They may use manipulation to control others and maintain their sense of superiority.
- **Experience Frequent Conflicts**: Their sense of entitlement and hypersensitivity to criticism can lead to frequent conflicts and strained relationships.

Implications for Work and Self-Identity

NPD also affects professional life and self-identity:

- **Workplace Dynamics**: In the workplace, individuals with NPD may exhibit both positive and negative behaviors. While their ambition and confidence can drive success, their arrogance and lack of teamwork can create a toxic work environment.
- **Self-Identity**: Individuals with NPD often have fragile self-esteem, despite outward appearances of confidence. Their self-identity heavily depends on external validation, making them vulnerable to feelings of emptiness and inadequacy when not receiving the admiration they crave.

Narcissistic Personality Disorder is a multifaceted condition with far-reaching implications for those affected by it and the people around them. By understanding the diagnostic criteria, the spectrum of narcissism, and the underlying psychological mechanisms, we can begin to comprehend the profound impact of NPD on relationships, work, and self-identity. This foundational knowledge sets the stage for exploring the origins, manifestations, and strategies for managing NPD in the subsequent chapters.

1.2 Historical Perspectives on Narcissism

The concept of narcissism has deep roots in mythology, literature, and psychological theory. Its evolution from a mythological tale to a well-defined psychological construct offers valuable insights into how our understanding of self-love and self-centeredness has developed over time. This chapter traces the historical perspectives on narcissism, from its origins in ancient mythology to its contemporary interpretation in psychological science.

Mythological Origins

The term "narcissism" originates from the Greek myth of Narcissus, a beautiful young man who fell in love with his reflection in a pool of water. According to the myth, Narcissus was so enamored with his image that he could not tear himself away, eventually perishing by the water's edge. This story, as recounted by the Roman poet Ovid in his work "Metamorphoses," symbolizes the dangers of excessive self-love and self-absorption.

The myth of Narcissus has endured through the centuries, serving as a cautionary tale about the perils of vanity and the inability to connect with others. It provides a vivid illustration of the core elements of narcissism: an intense preoccupation with oneself and a disregard for external reality.

Early Psychoanalytic Theories

The formal study of narcissism began with the advent of psychoanalysis in the late 19th and early 20th centuries. Sigmund Freud, the father of psychoanalysis, played a pivotal role in shaping our understanding of narcissism. In his seminal work "On Narcissism: An Introduction" (1914), Freud introduced the concept of narcissism as a normal stage of human development.

Freud proposed that individuals pass through a phase of primary narcissism during infancy, where they are entirely self-focused and see themselves as the center of the universe. As they grow, they gradually learn to invest their libidinal energy in external objects and people, a process known as "object love." However, in some individuals, this developmental process is disrupted, leading to pathological narcissism.

Freud distinguished between primary narcissism (a universal and healthy stage) and secondary narcissism (a pathological condition where the libido is withdrawn from external objects and reinvested in the self). He also linked narcissism to various mental health conditions, including schizophrenia and melancholia, suggesting that an exaggerated self-focus could lead to severe psychological disturbances.

Post-Freudian Developments

Following Freud, several psychoanalysts expanded on his theories and provided new insights into narcissism. Notably, Karen Horney and Heinz Kohut made significant contributions to the understanding of narcissism and its manifestations.

- **Karen Horney**: Horney challenged some of Freud's views, particularly his emphasis on biological drives. She emphasized the social and cultural factors in the development of narcissism. Horney introduced the concept of "basic anxiety," which arises from feelings of helplessness and insecurity during childhood. She argued that narcissistic behaviors could be seen as defensive strategies to cope with this anxiety and to gain a sense of safety and control.

- **Heinz Kohut**: Kohut's self-psychology theory provided a comprehensive framework for understanding narcissism. He introduced the idea of "narcissistic needs" and "self-objects"—people or things that individuals use to maintain their self-esteem. According to Kohut, healthy development involves the gradual internalization of self-objects, leading to a cohesive sense of self. When this process is disrupted, individuals may develop narcissistic personality structures as a way to compensate for their unmet needs.

Modern Perspectives

In the latter half of the 20th century, the study of narcissism expanded beyond psychoanalysis to include various psychological disciplines. Researchers began to explore narcissism through empirical studies, leading to a more nuanced understanding of its dimensions and impact.

- **Narcissistic Personality Inventory (NPI)**: Developed by Robert Raskin and Calvin S. Hall in 1979, the NPI is one of the most widely used tools for assessing narcissistic traits in non-clinical populations. It measures various aspects of narcissism, including authority, self-sufficiency, superiority, and exhibitionism.
- **Distinction between Grandiose and Vulnerable Narcissism**: Modern research has identified two primary forms of narcissism: grandiose and vulnerable. Grandiose narcissism is characterized by overt expressions of superiority, entitlement, and a need for admiration. In contrast, vulnerable narcissism involves hypersensitivity, defensiveness, and fragile self-esteem. This distinction has helped clarify the diverse manifestations of narcissistic traits and their underlying mechanisms.

Narcissism in Contemporary Society

The rise of social media and the digital age has brought new attention to narcissism, with some scholars suggesting that these platforms may encourage narcissistic behaviors by promoting self-promotion and instant gratification. The pervasive nature of social media has made it easier for individuals to seek validation and admiration from a wide audience, potentially exacerbating narcissistic tendencies.

However, it is important to recognize that not all social media use is indicative of narcissism. Researchers continue to investigate the complex relationship between digital culture and narcissistic behaviors, considering factors such as personality traits, social context, and individual motivations.

The historical perspectives on narcissism reveal a rich tapestry of ideas and theories that have shaped our understanding of this complex trait. From its mythological origins to its modern-day implications, narcissism has captivated the interest of scholars and clinicians alike. By tracing the evolution of narcissism through different theoretical lenses, we gain a deeper appreciation of its multifaceted nature and its profound impact on human behavior.

As we move forward in this book, we will build on these historical foundations to explore the contemporary understanding of narcissistic personality disorder, its manifestations, and its impact on various aspects of life. This historical context provides a valuable backdrop for our journey into the psychology of narcissism, helping us appreciate the enduring relevance of this fascinating and often enigmatic phenomenon.

1.3 Theories and Models of Narcissism

Understanding narcissism requires a deep dive into the various theories and models that have been proposed over the years. These theoretical frameworks offer diverse perspectives on the origins, mechanisms, and manifestations of narcissistic traits. In this chapter, we will explore the major theories and models of narcissism, ranging from classical psychoanalytic theories to contemporary psychological models.

Psychoanalytic Theories

Psychoanalytic theories have laid the groundwork for understanding narcissism as a complex psychological construct. The most influential contributions come from Sigmund Freud and subsequent psychoanalysts who expanded on his ideas.

Sigmund Freud

Freud's seminal work, "On Narcissism: An Introduction" (1914), introduced the concept of narcissism as a critical stage in human development. Freud distinguished between primary and secondary narcissism:

- **Primary Narcissism**: A normal developmental stage in infancy where the child's libido is invested in the self. During this phase, the infant's needs are met by caregivers, fostering a sense of omnipotence and self-importance.

- **Secondary Narcissism**: Occurs when an individual withdraws their libido from external objects and redirects it toward the self. This can result from experiences of frustration or loss, leading to a pathological state where self-love becomes excessive and maladaptive.

Freud also linked narcissism to various mental health conditions, suggesting that an exaggerated focus on the self could lead to psychosis and other severe psychological disorders.

Heinz Kohut

Heinz Kohut, a prominent figure in psychoanalysis, developed the self-psychology theory, which provides a comprehensive framework for understanding narcissism. Kohut introduced several key concepts:

- **Selfobjects**: People or things that individuals use to maintain their self-esteem and sense of self-cohesion. Healthy development involves the gradual internalization of self-objects, leading to a stable and cohesive self.
- **Narcissistic Needs**: According to Kohut, all individuals have narcissistic needs that must be met for healthy psychological development. These needs include mirroring (affirmation and validation), idealization (having someone to look up to), and twinship (a sense of belonging and sameness).
- **Fragmented Self**: When narcissistic needs are not adequately met, individuals may develop a fragmented self, characterized by feelings of emptiness, low self-esteem, and a reliance on external validation to maintain self-cohesion.

Kohut's theories emphasize the importance of early relationships in shaping narcissistic traits and highlight the potential for therapeutic interventions to address unmet narcissistic needs.

Contemporary Psychological Models

Modern psychological research has expanded the understanding of narcissism, incorporating empirical studies and diverse theoretical perspectives. Some of the most influential contemporary models include the distinction between grandiose and vulnerable narcissism and the Narcissistic Admiration and Rivalry Concept (NARC).

Grandiose and Vulnerable Narcissism

Contemporary research has identified two primary forms of narcissism: grandiose and vulnerable. These forms represent distinct manifestations of narcissistic traits and are associated with different underlying mechanisms and behavioral patterns.

- **Grandiose Narcissism**: Characterized by overt expressions of superiority, entitlement, and a need for admiration. Individuals with grandiose narcissism exhibit high self-confidence, assertiveness, and a tendency to seek out positions of power and recognition. They are often perceived as charming and charismatic but can also be manipulative and exploitative.
- **Vulnerable Narcissism**: Marked by hypersensitivity, defensiveness, and fragile self-esteem. Individuals with vulnerable narcissism may appear shy or introverted but harbor deep-seated

feelings of inadequacy and insecurity. They are highly sensitive to criticism and often experience intense emotional reactions to perceived slights or rejections.

This distinction has been crucial in refining diagnostic criteria and developing targeted interventions for different forms of narcissism.

Narcissistic Admiration and Rivalry Concept (NARC)

The Narcissistic Admiration and Rivalry Concept (NARC) is a contemporary model proposed by Back et al. (2013) that emphasizes two fundamental dimensions of narcissistic behavior:

- **Admiration**: Reflects the desire for social admiration and the pursuit of positive self-enhancement. Individuals high in narcissistic admiration seek to be admired and respected, often through charismatic and charming behavior. This dimension is associated with social dominance, assertiveness, and a focus on achieving success and recognition.
- **Rivalry**: Involves a competitive and antagonistic approach to social interactions. Individuals high in narcissistic rivalry strive to protect their self-esteem by devaluing and outcompeting others. This dimension is characterized by hostility, aggressiveness, and a tendency to perceive others as threats to their status and self-worth.

The NARC model highlights the dynamic interplay between self-promotion and self-protection strategies in narcissistic individuals, providing a nuanced understanding of how narcissistic traits manifest in different social contexts.

Cognitive-Behavioral Perspectives

Cognitive-behavioral theories focus on the role of thought patterns and behaviors in the development and maintenance of narcissistic traits. These perspectives emphasize the importance of cognitive distortions and maladaptive behaviors in shaping narcissistic personality features.

- **Cognitive Distortions**: Narcissistic individuals often exhibit cognitive distortions, such as overestimating their abilities, minimizing their flaws, and attributing failures to external factors. These distortions reinforce their grandiose self-image and protect their fragile self-esteem.
- **Maladaptive Behaviors**: Behaviors such as seeking constant validation, engaging in attention-seeking actions, and exploiting others serve to maintain the narcissistic individual's self-concept. Cognitive-behavioral interventions aim to address these behaviors by promoting more realistic self-appraisals and fostering healthier interpersonal interactions.

Evolutionary Perspectives

Evolutionary theories of narcissism propose that narcissistic traits may have evolved as adaptive strategies for social dominance and mate selection. These perspectives suggest that certain narcissistic behaviors, such as assertiveness and charm, may confer evolutionary advantages in specific social and environmental contexts.

- **Social Dominance**: Narcissistic traits such as confidence, assertiveness, and competitiveness may have evolved to help individuals attain higher social status and resources, enhancing their survival and reproductive success.
- **Mate Selection**: Traits associated with grandiose narcissism, such as physical attractiveness and social charm, may increase an individual's desirability as a mate, providing an evolutionary basis for the development and maintenance of these traits.

Evolutionary perspectives offer a broad understanding of why narcissistic traits persist in human populations and how they may be contextually adaptive.

Theories and models of narcissism provide a comprehensive framework for understanding the complex nature of this personality trait. From classical psychoanalytic theories to contemporary psychological models, each perspective offers unique insights into the origins, mechanisms, and manifestations of narcissistic traits. By integrating these diverse theoretical frameworks, we can develop a more nuanced understanding of narcissism and its impact on individuals and their relationships.

In the following chapters, we will build on these theoretical foundations to explore the real-world implications of narcissism, including its effects on personal relationships, professional environments, and self-identity. This theoretical background equips us with the tools to recognize, understand, and address narcissistic behaviors in various contexts.

1.4 Prevalence and Demographics

Understanding the prevalence and demographics of Narcissistic Personality Disorder (NPD) and narcissistic traits is crucial for appreciating the scope and impact of these phenomena on individuals and society. This section will explore the prevalence rates of NPD, variations across different populations, and demographic factors that influence the expression of narcissism.

Prevalence of Narcissistic Personality Disorder (NPD)

Narcissistic Personality Disorder is relatively uncommon compared to other personality disorders, but it still represents a significant mental health concern. Prevalence estimates vary depending on the criteria used for diagnosis and the populations studied.

- **General Population**: Epidemiological studies suggest that NPD affects approximately 1-6% of the general population. The wide range in prevalence estimates is partly due to differences in diagnostic methods and cultural variations in the expression of narcissistic traits.
- **Clinical Populations**: Among individuals receiving mental health treatment, the prevalence of NPD is higher, with estimates ranging from 2-16%. This higher prevalence in clinical settings may reflect the increased likelihood of individuals with severe symptoms seeking professional help.

Demographic Variations

The expression and prevalence of narcissistic traits and NPD can vary based on several demographic factors, including age, gender, culture, and socioeconomic status.

Age

Research indicates that narcissistic traits can fluctuate across the lifespan:

- **Young Adults**: Narcissistic traits are often more pronounced in adolescence and early adulthood. This stage of life is characterized by identity formation, self-exploration, and the pursuit of social validation, which can amplify narcissistic behaviors.
- **Middle Age and Older Adults**: As individuals age, they may experience a decrease in narcissistic traits. Factors such as increased life experience, greater emotional maturity, and changes in social roles can contribute to this decline. However, some studies suggest that certain aspects of narcissism, such as a desire for status and recognition, can persist into older adulthood.

Gender

Gender differences in the prevalence and expression of narcissistic traits and NPD have been consistently observed:

- **Men**: Studies generally find that men are more likely to be diagnosed with NPD than women. Men tend to exhibit higher levels of grandiose narcissism, characterized by assertiveness, dominance, and a desire for power and status.
- **Women**: While less common, women can also exhibit narcissistic traits, often manifesting as vulnerable narcissism. Women with narcissistic traits may display hypersensitivity, insecurity, and a greater need for approval and validation.

These gender differences may be influenced by socialization processes and cultural norms that shape how narcissistic behaviors are expressed and perceived.

Culture

Cultural factors play a significant role in shaping the prevalence and expression of narcissism. Different cultures have varying attitudes towards self-promotion, individualism, and social behavior:

- **Individualistic Cultures**: In cultures that emphasize individualism, such as the United States, there is a greater acceptance of self-promotion, assertiveness, and the pursuit of personal success. These cultural values can contribute to higher levels of narcissistic traits.
- **Collectivistic Cultures**: In contrast, collectivistic cultures, such as those in East Asia, prioritize group harmony, modesty, and interdependence. These cultural values may suppress overt expressions of narcissism, leading to lower prevalence rates or different manifestations of narcissistic traits.

Socioeconomic Status

Socioeconomic status (SES) can also influence the prevalence and expression of narcissistic traits:

- **Higher SES**: Individuals from higher socioeconomic backgrounds may have greater access to resources, opportunities for achievement, and social recognition, which can reinforce narcissistic behaviors. Additionally, the pursuit of wealth and status in affluent environments can promote narcissistic traits.
- **Lower SES**: In contrast, individuals from lower socioeconomic backgrounds may have fewer opportunities for self-promotion and validation. However, economic hardship and social marginalization can also lead to compensatory narcissistic behaviors as a means of coping with feelings of inadequacy and low self-worth.

Implications for Diagnosis and Treatment

Recognizing the prevalence and demographic variations of narcissistic traits and NPD has important implications for diagnosis and treatment:

- **Diagnostic Criteria**: Clinicians must consider cultural, gender, and socioeconomic factors when diagnosing NPD to avoid biases and ensure accurate assessments. Understanding these factors can help differentiate between culturally normative behaviors and pathological narcissism.

- **Tailored Interventions**: Treatment approaches should be tailored to address the specific needs and backgrounds of individuals with narcissistic traits or NPD. For example, interventions for young adults might focus on healthy identity formation and self-esteem, while treatments for older adults may address long-standing patterns of behavior and relationship dynamics.
- **Prevention and Education**: Public health initiatives and educational programs can promote awareness of narcissistic traits and their impact on well-being and relationships. By fostering emotional intelligence, empathy, and healthy self-esteem, these efforts can help mitigate the development of maladaptive narcissistic behaviors.

The prevalence and demographics of narcissism and NPD provide valuable insights into how these traits manifest across different populations and contexts. Understanding the variations in age, gender, culture, and socioeconomic status helps to create a more nuanced picture of narcissism and informs more effective diagnostic and therapeutic approaches.

As we continue to explore the complexities of narcissism, this knowledge will serve as a foundation for examining its impact on relationships, work, and self-identity. By considering the diverse factors that influence narcissistic traits, we can better understand the challenges and opportunities associated with addressing narcissism in various aspects of life.

Chapter 2: The Roots of Narcissism

Narcissism, particularly in its pathological form, often has deep-seated roots that can be traced back to early life experiences, genetic predispositions, and the influences of culture and society. This chapter delves into these foundational elements, exploring how various factors contribute to the development of narcissistic traits and Narcissistic Personality Disorder (NPD).

1. Early Childhood Experiences

Early childhood is a critical period for the formation of personality and self-concept. Several factors during this stage can significantly influence the development of narcissistic traits.

Parental Influence

The role of parents is paramount in shaping a child's self-esteem and self-perception. Several parenting styles and behaviors have been linked to the development of narcissistic traits:

- **Overvaluation and Excessive Praise**: When parents excessively praise their children, emphasizing their uniqueness and superiority, children may develop an inflated self-view. This can foster grandiose narcissism, characterized by a sense of entitlement and a need for admiration.

- **Neglect and Emotional Abuse**: Conversely, neglectful or emotionally abusive parenting can lead to vulnerable narcissism. Children who do not receive adequate emotional support may develop fragile self-esteem, seeking external validation to compensate for their feelings of inadequacy.
- **Inconsistent Parenting**: Inconsistency in parental behavior, where affection and attention are unpredictably given, can create confusion and insecurity in children. This inconsistency can lead to a heightened need for control and validation, traits often seen in narcissistic individuals.

Attachment Styles

Attachment theory provides another lens through which to understand the development of narcissism. Early attachment experiences with primary caregivers shape a child's ability to form healthy relationships later in life:

- **Secure Attachment**: Children with secure attachments generally develop healthy self-esteem and the capacity for empathy. They are less likely to develop narcissistic traits.
- **Insecure Attachment**: Insecure attachments, whether anxious or avoidant, can contribute to the development of narcissistic traits. Anxiously attached individuals may become overly dependent on external validation, while avoidantly attached individuals may develop a facade of self-sufficiency and superiority to protect against vulnerability.

2. Genetic and Biological Factors

While early experiences play a significant role, genetic and biological factors also contribute to the development of narcissistic traits and NPD.

Heritability of Narcissism

Research suggests that narcissistic traits have a genetic component. Twin studies have shown that there is a heritable basis for traits such as grandiosity and entitlement. This genetic predisposition can make individuals more susceptible to developing narcissistic traits when combined with environmental influences.

Neurobiological Factors

Neurobiological research has identified several brain regions and neural mechanisms associated with narcissism:

- **Prefrontal Cortex**: The prefrontal cortex, responsible for executive functions and self-regulation, has been found to differ in structure and function in individuals with high levels of narcissistic traits. Impairments in this region can lead to difficulties in empathy and impulse control.
- **Limbic System**: The limbic system, which regulates emotions, is also implicated in narcissism. Abnormalities in this system can contribute to emotional dysregulation, a common feature of vulnerable narcissism.

3. Cultural and Societal Influences

Cultural and societal factors play a crucial role in shaping the prevalence and expression of narcissistic traits. The values and norms of a society can either promote or inhibit narcissistic behaviors.

Individualism vs. Collectivism

Cultures can be broadly categorized as individualistic or collectivistic, and these orientations significantly impact the expression of narcissism:

- **Individualistic Cultures**: Societies that emphasize individual achievement, autonomy, and self-expression, such as the United States, tend to have higher levels of narcissism. These cultures often reward self-promotion and competition, which can reinforce narcissistic traits.
- **Collectivistic Cultures**: In contrast, collectivistic cultures, such as those in East Asia, prioritize group harmony, modesty, and interdependence. These values discourage overt narcissistic behaviors and promote more communal forms of self-esteem.

Media and Technology

The rise of social media and digital technology has created new platforms for self-expression and validation, potentially exacerbating narcissistic tendencies:

- **Social Media**: Platforms like Instagram, Facebook, and Twitter allow individuals to curate idealized versions of themselves and seek immediate validation through likes and comments. This environment can foster and amplify narcissistic behaviors, particularly among younger generations.
- **Reality Television and Celebrity Culture**: The glorification of fame and wealth in media can also contribute to the development of narcissistic traits. Reality television and celebrity culture often celebrate and reward narcissistic behaviors, making them more socially acceptable and desirable.

4. Psychodynamic and Cognitive-Behavioral Perspectives

Psychodynamic and cognitive-behavioral theories offer additional insights into the roots of narcissism, emphasizing the interplay between unconscious processes and learned behaviors.

Psychodynamic Theories

Psychodynamic theories, building on the work of Freud and his successors, emphasize the role of early relationships and unconscious conflicts in the development of narcissism:

- **Defense Mechanisms**: Narcissism can be seen as a defense mechanism to protect against deep-seated feelings of inadequacy and vulnerability. By constructing a grandiose self-image, individuals shield themselves from painful emotions and maintain a sense of control.

- **Object Relations Theory**: This theory focuses on the internalization of early relationships and how they shape the self. Disruptions in these early attachments can lead to a fragmented self-concept and the development of narcissistic defenses.

Cognitive-Behavioral Theories

Cognitive-behavioral theories highlight the role of thought patterns and learned behaviors in the development and maintenance of narcissistic traits:

- **Cognitive Distortions**: Individuals with narcissistic traits often engage in cognitive distortions, such as overestimating their abilities and underestimating others. These distorted thinking patterns reinforce their grandiose self-image and justify their entitlement.
- **Reinforcement and Conditioning**: Behaviors associated with narcissism, such as seeking admiration and attention, can be reinforced through social interactions. Positive reinforcement of these behaviors can lead to their persistence and escalation over time.

The roots of narcissism are multifaceted, involving a complex interplay of early childhood experiences, genetic and biological factors, cultural and societal influences, and psychological processes. By understanding these foundational elements, we can gain a deeper appreciation for the development of narcissistic traits and NPD.

As we move forward in this book, we will explore how these roots manifest in various aspects of life, including personal relationships, professional environments, and self-identity. This comprehensive understanding of the origins of narcissism provides a crucial backdrop for examining its impact and developing effective strategies for intervention and management.

2.1 Developmental Factors in Narcissism

Narcissistic traits often begin to manifest in early childhood and are significantly influenced by the quality of interactions and relationships during this formative period. Early developmental factors lay the groundwork for how individuals perceive themselves and others, shaping their interpersonal behaviors and emotional responses.

Early Childhood Experiences

Early childhood experiences, particularly interactions with primary caregivers, play a critical role in the development of narcissistic traits. These experiences can either foster healthy self-esteem and empathy or contribute to the formation of maladaptive narcissistic patterns.

Parental Influence:

Parental behaviors and parenting styles profoundly impact a child's sense of self-worth and interpersonal dynamics:

- **Overvaluation and Excessive Praise**: When caregivers consistently praise and overvalue their child's abilities, appearance, or achievements, it can cultivate an inflated sense of self-importance. Children internalize these messages, viewing themselves as exceptional and deserving of special treatment. This pattern is characteristic of grandiose narcissism, where individuals seek constant admiration and validation to maintain their elevated self-image.

- **Neglect and Emotional Deprivation**: Conversely, neglectful or emotionally unavailable parenting can lead to the development of vulnerable narcissism. Children who do not receive adequate emotional support may internalize feelings of worthlessness or insecurity. In response, they may develop a heightened sensitivity to criticism and a persistent need for external validation to counteract their perceived deficiencies.

- **Inconsistent Parenting Practices**: Inconsistency in parental behavior, where caregivers alternate between overly indulgent and neglectful responses, can contribute to confusion and emotional instability in children. This inconsistency may foster a reliance on external sources of validation and control as a means of coping with unpredictable environments.

Attachment Styles

Attachment theory provides a framework for understanding how early attachment experiences with caregivers influence emotional regulation and relationship dynamics throughout life:

- **Secure Attachment**: Children who develop secure attachments with caregivers typically experience consistent emotional support and responsiveness. They develop a stable sense of self-worth and trust in others, facilitating healthy interpersonal relationships characterized by empathy and reciprocity. Securely attached individuals are less likely to exhibit narcissistic traits, as they feel inherently valued and accepted.

- **Insecure Attachment**: Insecure attachment styles, such as anxious or avoidant attachments, can contribute to the development of narcissistic tendencies.

- **Anxious Attachment**: Children with anxious attachments may develop excessive reliance on external validation and approval to alleviate their fears of abandonment or rejection. This dependency on others' reassurance can manifest in narcissistic behaviors, such as attention-seeking and emotional volatility.

- **Avoidant Attachment**: Children with avoidant attachments may adopt a self-reliant and independent facade to protect themselves from perceived emotional threats. This self-sufficiency can evolve into a defensive form of narcissism, where individuals prioritize maintaining control and superiority to avoid vulnerability.

Psychological and Emotional Development

Beyond attachment styles, broader psychological and emotional development during childhood influences the expression of narcissistic traits:

- **Identity Formation**: The process of identity formation during adolescence and early adulthood is critical in shaping self-concept and interpersonal behaviors. Adolescents may experiment with different roles and identities, and those who receive consistently positive feedback for certain traits (e.g., intelligence, attractiveness) may internalize these attributes as central to their self-worth.

- **Emotional Regulation**: The ability to regulate emotions is crucial in determining how individuals respond to challenges and setbacks. Children who lack effective emotional regulation strategies may resort to narcissistic defenses, such as arrogance or denial of weaknesses, to protect their fragile self-esteem and maintain a sense of control.

Developmental factors in narcissism underscore the complex interplay between early experiences, attachment dynamics, and emotional development in shaping individuals' self-concept and interpersonal behaviors. Understanding these factors provides valuable insights into the origins of narcissistic traits and informs strategies for intervention and prevention.

As we continue to explore narcissism in subsequent chapters, we will examine how these developmental influences manifest in adult relationships, professional settings, and broader societal contexts. By addressing the roots of narcissism, we can foster healthier developmental pathways and promote more empathetic and authentic forms of self-expression and interpersonal engagement.

2.2 Genetic and Biological Influences

Genetic and biological factors contribute significantly to the development of narcissistic traits and Narcissistic Personality Disorder (NPD). This section explores the heritability of narcissism, neurobiological findings associated with narcissistic traits, and how these factors interact with environmental influences.

Heritability of Narcissism

Research suggests that narcissistic traits have a genetic component, indicating that certain personality characteristics and predispositions may be inherited from parents or ancestors. Twin and family studies have provided insights into the heritability of narcissism:

- **Twin Studies**: Studies comparing identical twins (who share 100% of their genes) and fraternal twins (who share approximately 50% of their genes) suggest that narcissistic traits are moderately heritable. For example, traits related to grandiosity, entitlement, and assertiveness show genetic influences.
- **Family Studies**: Family studies also support the heritability of narcissism, with traits such as self-centeredness and need for admiration observed across multiple generations. Familial transmission of narcissistic traits may involve genetic predispositions as well as learned behaviors and modeling from parental figures.

Neurobiological Factors

Neurobiological research has identified several brain regions and neural mechanisms associated with narcissism, providing insights into the neurobiological basis of this personality trait:

- **Prefrontal Cortex**: The prefrontal cortex, particularly the dorsolateral prefrontal cortex (DLPFC) and ventromedial prefrontal cortex (vmPFC), plays a crucial role in self-regulation, decision-making, and social cognition. Studies have shown structural and functional differences in these brain regions among individuals with narcissistic traits.

- **Structural Differences**: Individuals with narcissistic traits may exhibit alterations in prefrontal cortex structure, impacting their ability to regulate emotions and empathize with others.
- **Functional Differences**: Functional neuroimaging studies suggest that narcissistic individuals may show reduced activation in brain regions associated with empathy and perspective-taking, such as the anterior cingulate cortex (ACC) and temporoparietal junction (TPJ).
- **Limbic System**: The limbic system, which includes structures like the amygdala and hippocampus, is involved in emotional processing and regulation. Dysregulation within the limbic system may contribute to emotional volatility and sensitivity to criticism observed in narcissistic individuals.

Interaction of Genetic and Environmental Factors

While genetic predispositions play a significant role in the development of narcissistic traits, interactions with environmental factors are also crucial:

- **Gene-Environment Interactions**: Certain genetic predispositions may increase susceptibility to environmental influences, shaping the expression of narcissistic traits. For example, a genetic predisposition for high impulsivity combined with a permissive or neglectful parenting style may exacerbate narcissistic behaviors related to impulsiveness and entitlement.

- **Epigenetics**: Epigenetic mechanisms, which involve modifications to gene expression without altering the underlying DNA sequence, may also contribute to the development of narcissistic traits. Environmental factors such as early childhood experiences and stressors can influence epigenetic markers, potentially altering gene expression patterns associated with narcissism.

Evolutionary Perspectives

From an evolutionary standpoint, narcissistic traits may have adaptive advantages in certain contexts, such as social dominance and mate selection:

- **Social Dominance**: Narcissistic individuals may exhibit traits such as confidence, assertiveness, and charisma, which can enhance their ability to attain social status and resources within their social groups.
- **Mate Selection**: Certain narcissistic traits, such as physical attractiveness, charm, and self-assuredness, may increase an individual's desirability as a mate, potentially enhancing reproductive success in evolutionary terms.

Genetic and biological influences contribute to the complex etiology of narcissistic traits and NPD, interacting with environmental factors to shape individuals' self-concept, interpersonal behaviors, and emotional regulation. Understanding these influences provides valuable insights into the origins of narcissism and informs approaches to diagnosis, treatment, and prevention.

In the subsequent chapters, we will explore how these genetic and biological underpinnings intersect with developmental, cultural, and psychological factors to influence the manifestation and impact of narcissistic traits in various aspects of life. By integrating these multidimensional perspectives, we can enhance our understanding of narcissism and its implications for individuals and society.

2.3 Environmental and Social Contributors

Environmental and social factors play significant roles in shaping the development and expression of narcissistic traits. This section explores how cultural influences, societal norms, family dynamics, and other environmental factors contribute to the emergence and reinforcement of narcissistic behaviors.

Cultural and Societal Norms

Cultural values and societal norms significantly influence the prevalence and expression of narcissistic traits:

- **Individualism vs. Collectivism**: Cultures that emphasize individualism, such as those found in Western societies, tend to promote self-expression, personal achievement, and competition. These cultural values may encourage behaviors associated with grandiose narcissism, such as self-promotion, assertiveness, and pursuit of personal success.
- **Collectivism**: In contrast, cultures that prioritize collectivism, such as many East Asian societies, emphasize group harmony, modesty,

and cooperation. These cultural norms may discourage overt displays of narcissistic behaviors and instead foster communal forms of self-esteem and identity.

Family Dynamics

Family environments, including parental attitudes and dynamics, play a crucial role in the development of narcissistic traits:

- **Parental Overvaluation**: Parents who excessively praise their children, overemphasizing their specialness and superiority, may contribute to the development of grandiose narcissism. Children internalize these messages, forming inflated views of themselves and expecting constant admiration and validation from others.
- **Emotional Neglect or Abuse**: Emotional neglect or abuse, characterized by a lack of emotional responsiveness or harmful psychological interactions, can lead to the development of vulnerable narcissism. Children who experience emotional neglect may develop fragile self-esteem, seeking external validation to compensate for feelings of inadequacy or unworthiness.
- **Modeling and Reinforcement**: Children often model their behaviors after parental figures. If parents exhibit narcissistic traits themselves or engage in narcissistic behaviors (e.g., entitlement, lack of empathy), children may learn and replicate these behaviors as adaptive strategies for navigating interpersonal relationships.

Peer Influences

Peer relationships and social interactions also contribute to the development of narcissistic traits:

- **Peer Validation**: During adolescence and early adulthood, peers play a significant role in shaping self-concept and social behaviors. Individuals who receive validation and admiration from peers for certain traits (e.g., attractiveness, social skills) may internalize these qualities as central to their self-worth, potentially fostering narcissistic tendencies.
- **Social Media**: The advent of social media has provided new platforms for self-promotion, validation, and comparison. Individuals may curate idealized versions of themselves online, seeking validation through likes, comments, and followers. This environment can amplify narcissistic behaviors, particularly among younger generations.

Socioeconomic Influences

Socioeconomic status (SES) can impact the expression of narcissistic traits:

- **Higher SES**: Individuals from higher socioeconomic backgrounds may have greater access to resources, opportunities for achievement, and social recognition. The pursuit of success and status in affluent environments can reinforce narcissistic behaviors, such as entitlement and self-importance.

- **Lower SES**: In contrast, individuals from lower socioeconomic backgrounds may experience economic hardship and social marginalization, which can lead to compensatory narcissistic behaviors as a means of asserting control and maintaining self-esteem.

Cultural and Technological Trends

Cultural trends and technological advancements also influence the prevalence and manifestation of narcissistic traits:

- **Celebrity Culture and Reality Television**: The glorification of fame, wealth, and status in media, including reality television and celebrity culture, may contribute to the normalization and acceptance of narcissistic behaviors. Individuals exposed to these media portrayals may emulate narcissistic traits as desirable qualities for achieving success and recognition.
- **Digital Age and Self-Promotion**: The digital age has facilitated new forms of self-promotion and narcissistic expression through social media platforms and online communities. The ability to showcase achievements, experiences, and lifestyles to a wide audience can fuel narcissistic tendencies, particularly in contexts where validation and approval are readily accessible.

Environmental and social contributors play integral roles in shaping the development and expression of narcissistic traits. Cultural norms, family dynamics, peer influences, socioeconomic factors, and cultural trends all interact with individual predispositions to influence the manifestation of narcissism.

In subsequent chapters, we will explore how these environmental and social factors intersect with genetic, biological, and psychological influences to impact the course of narcissistic traits and Narcissistic Personality Disorder (NPD). By understanding these multidimensional influences, we can develop more comprehensive approaches to assessment, intervention, and support for individuals affected by narcissistic behaviors.

2.4 Childhood Experiences and Parenting Styles

Childhood experiences and parenting styles play crucial roles in shaping the development of narcissistic traits and Narcissistic Personality Disorder (NPD). This section explores how early interactions with caregivers, parental attitudes, and family dynamics contribute to the emergence and reinforcement of narcissistic behaviors.

Early Interactions with Caregivers

Early interactions with caregivers lay the foundation for emotional development and self-concept formation:

- **Attachment Theory**: According to attachment theory, the quality of attachment bonds between infants and caregivers influences socioemotional development. Secure attachments, characterized by responsive and emotionally attuned caregiving, promote healthy self-esteem and empathetic behavior. Insecure attachments, such as anxious or avoidant attachments, can contribute to the development of narcissistic traits.

- **Overvaluation and Praise**: Excessive praise and overvaluation from caregivers can inflate a child's sense of self-importance and entitlement. When children are consistently told they are superior or exceptional without realistic feedback, they may develop unrealistic expectations of entitlement and admiration from others.
- **Emotional Availability**: Caregivers who are emotionally available and responsive to a child's needs foster secure attachment bonds. Emotional unavailability, neglect, or inconsistent responses can lead to emotional dysregulation and a heightened need for external validation, characteristics often seen in narcissistic individuals.

Parenting Styles and Narcissistic Traits

Parenting styles significantly influence the development of narcissistic traits:

- **Authoritarian Parenting**: Authoritarian parenting, characterized by strict rules, harsh discipline, and low emotional warmth, may contribute to the development of narcissistic traits. Children raised under authoritarian parenting may develop a need for control, perfectionism, and a desire to assert dominance to compensate for perceived inadequacies.
- **Permissive Parenting**: Permissive parenting, which involves high levels of warmth but low levels of discipline and structure, can also foster narcissistic tendencies. Children may lack boundaries and develop a sense of entitlement, expecting others to meet their needs without considering the impact on others.
- **Authoritative Parenting**: Authoritative parenting, marked by high levels of warmth, responsiveness, and consistent discipline, promotes healthy emotional development and self-regulation.

Children raised with authoritative parenting tend to have secure attachments, develop empathy, and exhibit fewer narcissistic traits.

Family Dynamics and Role Modeling

Family dynamics and role modeling within the family unit can shape children's beliefs about themselves and others:

- **Siblings and Peer Relationships**: Interactions with siblings and peers provide opportunities for social learning and emotional regulation. Sibling rivalry or conflicts with peers can influence how children perceive their abilities and compare themselves to others, impacting self-esteem and narcissistic tendencies.
- **Parental Role Modeling**: Children often model behaviors observed in parental figures. If parents exhibit narcissistic traits, such as entitlement, lack of empathy, or grandiosity, children may internalize these behaviors as normative and emulate them in their relationships and interactions.

Cultural and Contextual Considerations

Cultural norms and societal expectations regarding parenting practices also influence the development of narcissistic traits:

- **Cultural Variations**: Cultural norms regarding individualism versus collectivism shape parenting practices and children's socialization experiences. Cultures that prioritize individual achievement and autonomy may inadvertently reinforce narcissistic behaviors, whereas collectivistic cultures may promote humility and interdependence.

- **Socioeconomic Factors**: Socioeconomic status (SES) can impact parenting styles and family dynamics. Higher SES families may have greater access to resources and opportunities for enrichment, influencing parenting practices that either mitigate or exacerbate narcissistic traits.

Childhood experiences and parenting styles significantly contribute to the development of narcissistic traits and NPD. Secure attachments, responsive caregiving, and authoritative parenting foster healthy emotional development and empathy, reducing the likelihood of narcissistic behaviors. In contrast, overvaluation, inconsistent parenting, and dysfunctional family dynamics can contribute to the emergence of narcissistic traits characterized by entitlement, lack of empathy, and a need for admiration.

In subsequent chapters, we will explore how these early experiences interact with genetic, neurobiological, and environmental factors to shape the course of narcissistic traits across the lifespan. Understanding these dynamics provides critical insights for intervention strategies and support systems aimed at promoting healthy socio-emotional development and reducing the impact of narcissistic behaviors on individuals and their relationships.

Chapter 3: Identifying Narcissistic Traits

In exploring narcissistic traits, it becomes evident that they manifest across a spectrum, influencing various aspects of individuals' lives and interactions. Understanding these traits involves a nuanced examination of their behavioral patterns, emotional undercurrents, and interpersonal dynamics.

Narcissistic Personality Disorder (NPD) is characterized by a pervasive pattern of grandiosity, a constant need for admiration, and a lack of empathy. These traits typically emerge in early adulthood and persist across different contexts, shaping individuals' perceptions of themselves and their interactions with others.

Characteristics of Narcissistic Traits

1. Grandiosity:

At the core of narcissistic traits lies a profound sense of grandiosity. Individuals with NPD often harbor fantasies of unlimited success, power, brilliance, or beauty. This grandiose self-image fuels their aspirations and expectations, driving them to seek positions and relationships that affirm their perceived superiority.

2. Need for Admiration:

A defining feature of narcissistic traits is the relentless pursuit of admiration and validation from others. Individuals with NPD crave constant reassurance of their special status and accomplishments. They may seek admiration through charm, achievements, or charismatic behavior, viewing others primarily as sources of affirmation.

3. Lack of Empathy:

Empathy, the ability to understand and share others' feelings, is notably lacking in individuals with narcissistic traits. They demonstrate an inability or unwillingness to recognize the emotions and perspectives of others, prioritizing their own needs and desires above those of others. This lack of empathy underpins their interpersonal interactions, often leading to disregard for others' boundaries or emotions.

Contextual Manifestations

Personal Relationships:

In personal relationships, narcissistic traits manifest in ways that can undermine intimacy and mutual respect. Individuals with NPD may exhibit manipulative behaviors to maintain control or admiration from their partners. They may idealize their partners initially, only to devalue them when they no longer serve their needs or expectations.

Professional Environments:

In professional settings, narcissistic traits may initially be perceived as strengths due to their assertiveness and self-confidence. However, these traits can contribute to interpersonal conflicts and organizational dysfunction. Individuals with NPD may prioritize their advancement and recognition, exhibiting a reluctance to collaborate or share credit with colleagues.

Social Interactions:

In social contexts, narcissistic individuals often seek attention and admiration through charismatic or dramatic behaviors. They may express a sense of entitlement and superiority over others, dismissing differing viewpoints or seeking relationships that enhance their social status. Their interactions may appear superficial, driven by the utility or perceived value of others.

Diagnostic Challenges

Diagnosing NPD presents challenges due to its complex presentation and the ego-syntonic nature of the disorder:

Ego-Syntonic Nature:

Individuals with NPD may not perceive their behaviors as problematic, viewing them as appropriate responses to their perceived exceptionalism. This ego-syntonic perspective complicates their willingness to seek or accept treatment, as they may resist acknowledging the impact of their behaviors on others.

Comorbidity and Differential Diagnosis:

NPD often co-occurs with other mental health conditions, such as depression, anxiety disorders, or substance use disorders. Clinicians must carefully differentiate between narcissistic traits and other personality disorders or mood disorders to develop tailored treatment plans.

Identifying narcissistic traits involves recognizing their multifaceted expressions across personal, professional, and social domains. By understanding the diagnostic criteria and contextual manifestations of narcissism, we can better navigate interactions with individuals exhibiting these traits and develop strategies for intervention and support. In the subsequent chapters, we will explore the impact of narcissistic traits on relationships, self-identity, and psychological well-being, providing insights into effective approaches for managing and mitigating their effects.

3.1 Characteristics of Narcissistic Personality Disorder

Narcissistic Personality Disorder (NPD) is defined by a constellation of enduring patterns of behavior, cognition, and interpersonal functioning. These characteristics collectively contribute to a pervasive sense of grandiosity, a constant need for admiration, and a lack of empathy. Understanding the specific traits of NPD provides insights into its diagnostic criteria and the impact it has on individuals' lives.

Core Characteristics

1. Grandiosity:

Central to NPD is an inflated sense of self-importance and superiority. Individuals with NPD often exaggerate their achievements, talents, or abilities, viewing themselves as inherently special and deserving of privileged treatment. This grandiose self-image is accompanied by fantasies of unlimited success, power, brilliance, or beauty.

2. Need for Admiration:

A hallmark feature of NPD is the relentless pursuit of admiration and validation from others. Individuals with NPD crave constant reassurance of their superiority and may seek admiration through attention-seeking behaviors, boasting, or demanding special treatment. The need for admiration fuels their self-esteem and serves as a primary motivation in their interactions.

3. Lack of Empathy:

Empathy, the ability to understand and share others' feelings, is notably deficient in individuals with NPD. They demonstrate a profound inability or unwillingness to recognize the emotions, perspectives, and needs of others. This lack of empathy leads to interpersonal difficulties, as they prioritize their desires and disregard the impact of their behavior on others.

4. Sense of Entitlement:

Individuals with NPD often exhibit an entitled attitude, believing they are inherently deserving of favorable treatment from others. They may expect special privileges, admiration, or compliance without considering reciprocal obligations or the perspectives of others. This sense of entitlement underpins their interactions and contributes to feelings of frustration or resentment when their expectations are not met.

5. Exploitative Behavior:

In interpersonal relationships, individuals with NPD may exploit others to achieve their own goals or gratification. They may manipulate or deceive others to maintain control or admiration, using charm, flattery, or intimidation to achieve their desired outcomes. Exploitative behaviors reflect a lack of ethical considerations or empathy for the well-being of others.

6. Interpersonal Difficulties:

Due to their narcissistic traits, individuals with NPD often experience tumultuous interpersonal relationships characterized by conflict, manipulation, idealization, and devaluation cycles. Their interactions may be superficial or transactional, driven by their need for admiration or validation rather than genuine emotional connection.

Diagnostic Criteria and Considerations

Diagnosing NPD requires a comprehensive evaluation of these core characteristics and their impact on various aspects of an individual's life. The Diagnostic and Statistical Manual of Mental Disorders (DSM-5) outlines specific criteria for diagnosing NPD, emphasizing the enduring nature of these traits and their impairment in functioning:

- **Diagnostic Criteria**: The DSM-5 criteria for NPD include a pervasive pattern of grandiosity, need for admiration, and lack of empathy, beginning by early adulthood and present in a variety of contexts. The disorder significantly impacts interpersonal relationships, occupational functioning, and overall well-being.
- **Differential Diagnosis**: Clinicians must differentiate NPD from other personality disorders, mood disorders, or behavioral patterns that may share overlapping symptoms. Comorbid conditions, such as depression or substance use disorders, can complicate diagnosis and treatment planning.

The characteristics of Narcissistic Personality Disorder encompass a complex interplay of grandiosity, entitlement, lack of empathy, and interpersonal difficulties. By understanding these core features, clinicians can accurately assess and diagnose NPD, providing individuals with appropriate interventions and support. In the subsequent chapters, we will explore the impact of NPD on relationships, self-identity, and treatment approaches aimed at addressing the challenges associated with narcissistic traits.

3.2 Diagnostic Criteria and Assessment Tools

Diagnosing Narcissistic Personality Disorder (NPD) involves a systematic evaluation of specific criteria outlined in the Diagnostic and Statistical Manual of Mental Disorders (DSM-5). Additionally, various assessment tools and clinical approaches aid in identifying and understanding the complex nature of NPD.

Diagnostic Criteria for NPD

The DSM-5 outlines specific criteria for diagnosing NPD, focusing on enduring patterns of behavior, cognition, and interpersonal functioning. To meet the criteria for NPD, an individual must exhibit significant impairments in self-functioning and interpersonal functioning across the following domains:

- **Grandiosity**: A pervasive pattern of grandiosity, characterized by fantasies of unlimited success, power, brilliance, or beauty.
- **Need for Admiration**: A constant need for admiration and excessive admiration-seeking behavior.
- **Lack of Empathy**: A lack of empathy, is demonstrated by an inability or unwillingness to recognize the feelings and needs of others.
- **Interpersonal Exploitation**: Engaging in exploitative behaviors to achieve their own goals, often at the expense of others' well-being.
- **Sense of Entitlement**: A sense of entitlement, expecting special treatment or compliance with their expectations.

- **Arrogance or Haughty Attitudes**: Displaying arrogant behaviors or attitudes, characterized by a belief in their superiority and entitlement.

Assessment Tools for NPD

Several standardized assessment tools and clinical interviews aid in diagnosing and assessing NPD:

- **Structured Clinical Interview for DSM Disorders (SCID)**: The SCID is a widely used diagnostic interview that guides clinicians through a structured assessment of DSM-5 criteria for personality disorders, including NPD.
- **Personality Diagnostic Questionnaire (PDQ-4)**: The PDQ-4 is a self-report questionnaire designed to assess personality disorders, including NPD, based on DSM criteria.
- **Millon Clinical Multiaxial Inventory (MCMI-IV)**: The MCMI-IV includes scales for assessing personality disorders, providing clinicians with information about pathological personality traits and patterns associated with NPD.
- **Clinical Observation and History Taking**: Comprehensive clinical assessments often involve gathering information from multiple sources, including direct observation, collateral reports from family members or colleagues, and a thorough review of the individual's developmental history and current functioning.

Challenges in Diagnosis

Diagnosing NPD can be challenging due to several factors:

- **Ego-Syntonic Nature**: Individuals with NPD may not perceive their behaviors as problematic, making self-report unreliable and necessitating collateral information from others.
- **Comorbidity**: NPD often co-occurs with other mental health conditions, such as depression, anxiety disorders, or substance use disorders, complicating diagnosis and treatment planning.
- **Stigma and Resistance to Diagnosis**: The stigma associated with personality disorders and the reluctance of individuals with NPD to acknowledge their symptoms can hinder accurate diagnosis and engagement in treatment.

Diagnosing Narcissistic Personality Disorder involves a careful assessment of specific DSM-5 criteria and the use of standardized assessment tools and clinical interviews. By understanding the diagnostic criteria and challenges associated with diagnosing NPD, clinicians can develop effective treatment plans tailored to address the unique needs and impairments of individuals with this disorder. In the subsequent chapters, we will explore treatment approaches and interventions aimed at managing narcissistic traits and promoting positive outcomes for individuals affected by NPD.

3.3 Differentiating Narcissism from Other Personality Disorders

Understanding how Narcissistic Personality Disorder (NPD) differs from other personality disorders is essential for accurate diagnosis and effective treatment planning. While there may be overlapping symptoms and behaviors among various personality disorders, each disorder is characterized by distinct features and patterns of maladaptive behavior.

Borderline Personality Disorder (BPD)

Borderline Personality Disorder shares some similarities with NPD, particularly in terms of unstable self-image and intense interpersonal relationships. However, key differences include:

- **Core Features**: BPD is characterized by unstable self-image, intense and unstable relationships, impulsivity, and recurrent suicidal behavior or self-mutilation. Individuals with BPD often experience chronic feelings of emptiness and have difficulty controlling anger.
- **Interpersonal Relationships**: While individuals with both BPD and NPD may exhibit intense and stormy relationships, those with BPD tend to experience fear of abandonment and exhibit more reactive emotional responses compared to the more stable and grandiose sense of self in NPD.

Antisocial Personality Disorder (ASPD)

Antisocial Personality Disorder overlaps with NPD in terms of disregard for others' rights and feelings, but differs significantly in motivation and behavioral patterns:

- **Core Features**: ASPD is characterized by a pervasive pattern of disregard for and violation of the rights of others. Individuals with ASPD may engage in criminal behavior, deceitfulness, impulsivity, and a lack of remorse.
- **Motivation**: While individuals with NPD may manipulate others to maintain a grandiose self-image and obtain admiration, those with ASPD manipulate others primarily for personal gain or to fulfill immediate desires, often without consideration for the consequences.

Histrionic Personality Disorder (HPD)

Histrionic Personality Disorder shares some similarities with NPD in terms of seeking attention and admiration, but differs in the underlying motivations and emotional expression:

- **Core Features**: HPD is characterized by excessive emotionality and attention-seeking behavior. Individuals with HPD may exhibit a dramatic expression of emotions, shallow relationships, and a strong desire to be the center of attention.
- **Motivation**: While individuals with NPD seek admiration to affirm their grandiose self-image and superiority, those with HPD

seek attention and approval to alleviate feelings of emptiness and insecurity, often without the entitlement or lack of empathy seen in NPD.

Avoidant Personality Disorder (AvPD)

Avoidant Personality Disorder contrasts with NPD in terms of self-perception and interpersonal behavior:

- **Core Features**: AvPD is characterized by social inhibition, feelings of inadequacy, and hypersensitivity to negative evaluation. Individuals with AvPD avoid social interactions and fear rejection or criticism.
- **Interpersonal Behavior**: While individuals with NPD may exhibit arrogance and a sense of entitlement in interpersonal interactions, those with AvPD tend to withdraw from relationships and avoid situations where they might be judged or criticized, reflecting underlying feelings of inferiority rather than superiority.

Differentiating Narcissistic Personality Disorder from other personality disorders involves understanding the unique features and patterns of maladaptive behavior associated with each disorder. While there may be overlapping symptoms, such as interpersonal difficulties or emotional dysregulation, the motivations, self-perceptions, and interpersonal dynamics distinguish NPD from Borderline, Antisocial, Histrionic, and Avoidant Personality Disorders. A comprehensive assessment, including clinical interviews and standardized assessment tools, is essential for accurate diagnosis and effective treatment planning tailored to the individual's specific needs and impairments.

3.4 Subtypes of Narcissism: Grandiose vs. Vulnerable

Narcissistic Personality Disorder (NPD) encompasses two main subtypes: grandiose narcissism and vulnerable narcissism. These subtypes reflect different expressions of narcissistic traits and underlying psychological mechanisms, influencing how individuals with NPD interact with others and perceive themselves.

Grandiose Narcissism

Characteristics:

Grandiose narcissism is characterized by an exaggerated sense of self-importance, entitlement, and a need for admiration. Individuals with grandiose narcissism often display:

- **Grandiosity**: A pervasive pattern of grandiosity, marked by fantasies of unlimited success, power, brilliance, or beauty. They may exaggerate their achievements and talents, believing they are superior to others.
- **Need for Admiration**: A constant need for admiration and validation from others to maintain their inflated self-image. They seek praise, admiration, and special treatment, viewing others primarily as sources of affirmation.
- **Lack of Empathy**: A notable lack of empathy and disregard for the feelings and needs of others. They may exploit others to achieve their own goals or gratification, demonstrating manipulative behaviors without guilt or remorse.

- **Interpersonal Style**: Grandiose narcissists often exhibit charm, charisma, and assertiveness in social interactions. They may dominate conversations, seek leadership roles, and expect to be the center of attention.
- **Emotional Regulation**: They may have difficulty regulating emotions, especially in response to perceived criticism or challenges to their self-image. Criticism or failure may trigger feelings of anger, shame, or humiliation.

Vulnerable Narcissism

Characteristics:

Vulnerable narcissism, also known as covert or fragile narcissism, differs from grandiose narcissism in its outward presentation and underlying insecurities. Individuals with vulnerable narcissism exhibit:

- **Insecurity and Hypersensitivity**: Unlike grandiose narcissists who project confidence, individuals with vulnerable narcissism often experience underlying feelings of insecurity, inadequacy, and hypersensitivity to criticism or rejection.
- **Grandiosity under Threat**: While they may not openly display grandiosity, vulnerable narcissists harbor fantasies of success or special achievements. They may react defensively to perceived threats to their self-esteem or self-worth.
- **Entitlement and Self-Pity**: They may feel entitled to special treatment or recognition but express this entitlement through self-pity or passive-aggressive behaviors rather than overt arrogance.

- **Social Withdrawal**: Vulnerable narcissists may avoid situations that could potentially expose their vulnerabilities or trigger feelings of shame. They may struggle with forming deep, meaningful relationships due to fear of rejection or criticism.
- **Covert Manipulation**: Instead of overtly seeking admiration, vulnerable narcissists may manipulate others subtly to fulfill their emotional needs or validate their self-worth. They may play the victim or elicit sympathy from others to bolster their fragile self-esteem.

Relationship Dynamics

- **Grandiose Narcissism**: In relationships, grandiose narcissists may seek partners who admire and validate their superiority. They may dominate relationships and expect their partners to fulfill their needs without reciprocation.
- **Vulnerable Narcissism**: Individuals with vulnerable narcissism may form dependent or tumultuous relationships characterized by emotional volatility and fear of abandonment. They may struggle with intimacy and trust, fearing exposure of their insecurities.

Treatment Implications

Understanding these subtypes informs treatment approaches for NPD:

- **Grandiose Narcissism**: Interventions focus on challenging grandiose beliefs, improving empathy and interpersonal skills, and addressing emotional regulation. Cognitive-behavioral therapy (CBT) and psychodynamic therapy may be effective.

- **Vulnerable Narcissism**: Therapy aims to address underlying insecurities, enhance self-esteem, and develop healthier coping mechanisms for managing feelings of inadequacy and fear of rejection. Emotion-focused therapies and supportive psychotherapy can be beneficial.

The distinction between grandiose and vulnerable narcissism highlights the diverse manifestations of NPD and their impact on individuals' functioning and relationships. Recognizing these subtypes guides clinicians in tailoring interventions that address specific traits, emotional vulnerabilities, and interpersonal challenges associated with each subtype of narcissism. In the subsequent chapters, we will explore treatment approaches and strategies aimed at promoting self-awareness, empathy, and healthy relationship dynamics for individuals affected by NPD.

Chapter 4: Narcissism in Relationships

Narcissism profoundly influences interpersonal relationships, shaping dynamics in both personal and professional contexts. This chapter explores how Narcissistic Personality Disorder (NPD) manifests within relationships, impacting communication patterns, emotional dynamics, and overall relationship satisfaction.

Impact on Communication

Individuals with Narcissistic Personality Disorder often exhibit distinct communication patterns that reflect their grandiose self-image and need for admiration:

1. **Dominance and Control**: Narcissists may dominate conversations, steering discussions toward topics that highlight their achievements or strengths. They may dismiss others' contributions or opinions that do not align with their views.
2. **Self-Centeredness**: Communication with narcissists often revolves around their own experiences, desires, and achievements. They may show limited interest in others' perspectives or emotions unless it relate directly to their agenda.
3. **Manipulation and Gaslighting**: Narcissists may use manipulation tactics, such as gaslighting, to distort reality and undermine others' perceptions. They may deny facts, minimize others' experiences, or blame others for conflicts to maintain their self-image.

Emotional Dynamics

Narcissistic traits significantly impact emotional dynamics within relationships, often leading to instability and conflict:

1. **Lack of Empathy**: Empathy deficits in narcissists contribute to difficulties in understanding and responding to their partner's emotions. They may invalidate or dismiss their partner's feelings, prioritizing their own emotional needs.
2. **Idealization and Devaluation**: Narcissists may idealize their partner during the initial stages of a relationship, viewing them as perfect and meeting their needs for admiration. Over time, they may devalue their partner if they perceive them as failing to meet their unrealistic expectations.
3. **Emotional Regulation Challenges**: Narcissists may struggle with regulating their emotions, reacting strongly to perceived criticism or rejection. They may exhibit anger, defensiveness, or withdrawal when their self-esteem is threatened.

Relationship Satisfaction and Dynamics

The presence of narcissistic traits can significantly impact overall relationship satisfaction and stability:

1. **Power Imbalance**: Relationships with narcissists often involve a power imbalance, where the narcissist seeks control and admiration while their partner may feel subordinate or undervalued.

2. **Dependency vs. Independence**: Partners of narcissists may oscillate between dependency on the narcissist for validation and independence as they navigate the emotional volatility and unpredictability of the relationship.
3. **Cycle of Idealization and Devaluation**: Narcissistic relationships may cycle between periods of idealization, where the partner feels cherished and valued, and devaluation, where they experience criticism, emotional withdrawal, or neglect.

Coping Strategies for Partners

Navigating a relationship with a narcissist requires self-awareness and adaptive coping strategies:

1. **Setting Boundaries**: Establishing clear boundaries can help mitigate manipulation and maintain emotional well-being within the relationship.
2. **Seeking Support**: Seeking support from friends, family, or a therapist can provide validation and perspective outside of the narcissistic dynamic.
3. **Self-Care**: Prioritizing self-care, maintaining hobbies and interests, and fostering personal growth can strengthen resilience and autonomy within the relationship.

Narcissism profoundly influences interpersonal dynamics and relationship satisfaction, impacting communication patterns, emotional dynamics, and power dynamics within relationships. Recognizing the effects of Narcissistic Personality Disorder on relationships provides insights into developing strategies for communication, emotional regulation, and maintaining personal well-being. In the subsequent chapters, we will explore interventions and therapeutic approaches aimed at improving relationship outcomes and promoting healthier interactions for individuals affected by NPD and their partners.

4.1 The Narcissistic Partner: Signs and Dynamics

Navigating a relationship with a narcissistic partner involves understanding distinctive signs and dynamics that characterize their behavior and interactions. This section explores common traits and dynamics associated with narcissistic partners, shedding light on the complexities of such relationships.

Signs of a Narcissistic Partner

1. Grandiose Self-Image:

Narcissistic partners often exhibit an exaggerated sense of self-importance and superiority. They may constantly seek admiration and validation from others, emphasizing their achievements or unique qualities.

2. Lack of Empathy:

Empathy deficits are hallmark traits of narcissistic individuals. They may struggle to recognize or respond sensitively to their partner's emotions, prioritizing their own needs and desires.

3. Manipulative Behavior:

Narcissists may engage in manipulative tactics to maintain control or gain an advantage in the relationship. This can include gaslighting (distorting facts or reality), guilt-tripping, or using charm to manipulate emotions.

4. Boundary Violations:

Boundary violations are common in relationships with narcissistic partners. They may disregard their partner's boundaries, insist on their agenda, or dismiss their partner's needs.

5. Intermittent Reinforcement:

Narcissistic partners often employ intermittent reinforcement, alternating between affection and criticism. This cycle of idealization and devaluation can confuse their partner and perpetuate emotional dependence.

Dynamics in the Relationship

1. Power Imbalance:

Narcissistic relationships typically exhibit a power imbalance where the narcissistic partner seeks control and admiration while their partner may feel subordinate or undervalued. Decisions and interactions may revolve around meeting the narcissist's needs and maintaining their self-image.

2. Emotional Rollercoaster:

Relationships with narcissistic partners can be emotionally volatile. The partner may experience intense highs during periods of idealization, followed by profound lows during devaluation phases characterized by criticism, emotional withdrawal, or neglect.

3. Dependency and Isolation:

Partners of narcissists may oscillate between dependency on the narcissist for validation and independence as they navigate the unpredictable dynamics of the relationship. Narcissists may isolate their partners from supportive networks to maintain control and dependency.

4. Emotional Manipulation:

Narcissistic partners may manipulate emotions to maintain dominance and control. They may use emotional outbursts, guilt-tripping, or passive-aggressive behaviors to elicit specific reactions or maintain their partner's focus on meeting their needs.

Impact on the Partner

Navigating a relationship with a narcissistic partner can have profound emotional and psychological effects on the partner:

1. Emotional Exhaustion:

Constantly managing the narcissist's emotions and demands can lead to emotional exhaustion for the partner. They may feel drained from navigating the unpredictable dynamics and trying to meet unrealistic expectations.

2. Low Self-Esteem:

Narcissistic relationships can erode the partner's self-esteem and self-worth. Constant criticism or comparison to idealized standards set by the narcissist can undermine their confidence and sense of identity.

3. Isolation and Alienation:

Narcissistic partners may isolate their partners from supportive networks or activities that promote independence. This isolation can further entrench dependency on the narcissist and limit opportunities for outside perspective or support.

Coping Strategies for Partners

Navigating a relationship with a narcissistic partner requires self-awareness and adaptive coping strategies:

1. Setting Boundaries:

Establishing clear boundaries is essential for maintaining emotional well-being and asserting personal needs within the relationship.

2. Seeking Support:

Seeking support from friends, family, or a therapist can provide validation, perspective, and strategies for managing the challenges of a narcissistic relationship.

3. Self-Care:

Prioritizing self-care, engaging in hobbies or activities that promote personal well-being, and fostering independence can strengthen resilience and autonomy within the relationship.

Understanding the signs and dynamics of a relationship with a narcissistic partner provides insight into the challenges faced by individuals in such relationships. Recognizing the impact of narcissistic behavior on emotional dynamics and self-esteem empowers partners to implement strategies for maintaining personal well-being and navigating complex interpersonal dynamics. In the subsequent chapters, we will explore interventions and approaches aimed at improving relationship outcomes and promoting healthier interactions for partners of individuals affected by Narcissistic Personality Disorder.

4.2 Impact on Romantic Relationships

Narcissistic Personality Disorder (NPD) profoundly influences romantic relationships, shaping dynamics that impact both partners' emotional well-being and relationship satisfaction. This section explores the specific impact of NPD on romantic relationships, highlighting key dynamics and challenges faced by partners of individuals with narcissistic traits.

Dynamics of Romantic Relationships with a Narcissistic Partner

1. Idealization and Devaluation:

Narcissistic partners often engage in a cycle of idealization and devaluation. Initially, they may idealize their partner, showering them with attention, admiration, and affection. However, as the relationship progresses, they may begin to devalue their partner, criticizing or devaluing their contributions, appearance, or behaviors.

2. Emotional Manipulation:

Narcissistic individuals may use emotional manipulation tactics to maintain control and dominance in the relationship. This can include gaslighting (distorting reality or denying facts), guilt-tripping, or playing the victim to garner sympathy and manipulate their partner's emotions.

3. Lack of Empathy and Emotional Intimacy:

Empathy deficits are characteristic of NPD, leading to challenges in emotional intimacy within romantic relationships. Narcissistic partners may struggle to understand or respond to their partner's emotions, focusing primarily on their own needs and desires.

4. Power Imbalance:

Narcissistic relationships often exhibit a significant power imbalance, where the narcissistic partner seeks admiration, compliance, and validation while their partner may feel subordinate or undervalued. Decision-making and relationship dynamics may revolve around meeting the narcissist's needs and maintaining their self-image.

Impact on the Non-Narcissistic Partner

1. Emotional Exhaustion and Stress:

Navigating a relationship with a narcissistic partner can be emotionally exhausting and stressful for the non-narcissistic partner. Constantly managing the narcissist's emotions, demands, and expectations can lead to burnout and feelings of overwhelm.

2. Low Self-Esteem and Self-Worth:

Criticism, manipulation, and comparison to idealized standards set by the narcissistic partner can erode the non-narcissistic partner's self-esteem and self-worth. They may internalize the narcissist's negative messages, doubting their abilities and value within the relationship.

3. Isolation and Alienation:

Narcissistic partners may isolate their romantic partners from supportive networks or activities that promote independence. This isolation can increase dependency on the narcissistic partner and limit opportunities for outside perspective or support.

4. Difficulty Establishing Boundaries:

Maintaining boundaries in a relationship with a narcissistic partner can be challenging. The narcissist may disregard their partner's boundaries, insisting on their agenda or dismissing their partner's needs, which can lead to feelings of frustration and powerlessness.

Long-Term Relationship Patterns

1. Cycling Between Intimacy and Distance:

Narcissistic relationships often cycle between moments of intense intimacy during idealization phases and emotional distance or conflict during devaluation phases. This pattern can create instability and unpredictability in the relationship.

2. Persistent Relationship Strain:

Over time, the strain of navigating a relationship with a narcissistic partner can lead to persistent relationship dissatisfaction and conflict. The non-narcissistic partner may feel unfulfilled or trapped in a cycle of emotional turmoil and uncertainty.

3. Impact on Future Relationships:

Partners of individuals with NPD may carry emotional wounds and relational patterns into future relationships. They may struggle with trust, intimacy, and setting boundaries, impacting their ability to form healthy and fulfilling relationships.

Coping Strategies for Partners

Navigating a romantic relationship with a narcissistic partner requires adaptive coping strategies and self-care practices:

1. Setting Clear Boundaries:

Establishing and maintaining clear boundaries is crucial for protecting emotional well-being and asserting personal needs within the relationship.

2. Seeking Support:

Seeking support from friends, family, or a therapist can provide validation, perspective, and strategies for managing the challenges of a narcissistic relationship.

3. Focusing on Self-Care:

Prioritizing self-care, engaging in activities that promote personal well-being and fulfillment, and fostering independence outside of the relationship can strengthen resilience and autonomy.

Narcissistic Personality Disorder significantly impacts romantic relationships, influencing dynamics such as idealization, emotional manipulation, power imbalances, and emotional intimacy. Understanding the specific challenges faced by partners of individuals with NPD empowers individuals to implement strategies for maintaining emotional well-being, setting boundaries, and navigating complex interpersonal dynamics. In the subsequent chapters, we will explore interventions and therapeutic approaches aimed at improving relationship outcomes and promoting healthier interactions for partners affected by NPD.

4.3 Narcissistic Parenting: Effects on Children

Parental narcissism can profoundly impact children's emotional development, self-esteem, and overall well-being. This section explores the effects of narcissistic parenting on children, highlighting common dynamics and long-term consequences observed in such family environments.

Dynamics of Narcissistic Parenting

1. Lack of Empathy and Emotional Support:

Narcissistic parents often struggle with empathy and emotional attunement to their children's needs. They may prioritize their desires, achievements, or emotional demands over their children's emotional well-being, leading to feelings of neglect or emotional abandonment.

2. Unrealistic Expectations and Pressures:

Narcissistic parents may impose unrealistic expectations on their children to reflect positively on the parent's image or fulfill unmet ambitions. These expectations can be unreasonably high and may not align with the child's developmental stage or personal interests.

3. Conditional Love and Validation:

Children of narcissistic parents often experience love and validation as conditional upon meeting the parent's expectations or mirroring the parent's desires and achievements. They may feel valued only when they fulfill the parent's needs for admiration or validation.

4. Gaslighting and Manipulation:

Narcissistic parents may use gaslighting tactics to manipulate their children's perceptions of reality or undermine their self-confidence. They may deny or distort the child's experiences, feelings, or achievements to maintain control or protect their self-image.

Impact on Children

1. Low Self-Esteem and Self-Worth:

Growing up in an environment where their needs and emotions are invalidated can lead children of narcissistic parents to develop low self-esteem and self-worth. They may internalize the message that their value is contingent upon meeting external expectations or standards.

2. Emotional Dysregulation:

Children of narcissistic parents may struggle with emotional dysregulation, experiencing difficulty in identifying and managing their emotions. They may suppress emotions to avoid parental disapproval or exhibit heightened emotional reactivity in response to stress or conflict.

3. Difficulty Establishing Boundaries:

Boundary violations in narcissistic parenting can make it challenging for children to establish healthy boundaries in relationships. They may struggle with assertiveness, feel responsible for managing parental emotions, or have difficulty recognizing their own needs and preferences.

4. Intergenerational Transmission of Narcissism:

Children of narcissistic parents may internalize narcissistic traits or relational patterns, perpetuating intergenerational cycles of narcissism in their own relationships and parenting styles.

Long-Term Consequences

1. Impaired Interpersonal Relationships:

Adult children of narcissistic parents may experience challenges in forming and maintaining healthy interpersonal relationships. They may struggle with trust, intimacy, and vulnerability, fearing rejection or abandonment similar to their experiences in childhood.

2. Emotional Vulnerability and Mental Health Issues:

The emotional toll of narcissistic parenting can contribute to long-term mental health issues, such as anxiety, depression, or personality disorders. Children may carry unresolved emotional wounds into adulthood, impacting their overall well-being and quality of life.

3. Achievement Orientation and Perfectionism:

Children raised by narcissistic parents may adopt an achievement-oriented mindset or perfectionistic tendencies as a coping mechanism to gain parental approval or avoid criticism. This can lead to chronic stress, burnout, or dissatisfaction despite external success.

Coping Strategies for Adult Children

Navigating the legacy of narcissistic parenting as an adult child requires self-awareness and intentional healing strategies:

1. Self-Reflection and Therapy:

Engaging in self-reflection and seeking therapy can help adult children of narcissistic parents process their experiences, identify patterns of behavior, and develop healthier coping strategies for managing emotions and relationships.

2. Setting Boundaries:

Establishing and maintaining clear boundaries in relationships, particularly with narcissistic parents, is crucial for protecting emotional well-being and asserting personal needs.

3. Building Supportive Relationships:

Cultivating supportive relationships with friends, partners, or support groups can provide validation, empathy, and perspective outside of the narcissistic family dynamic.

Narcissistic parenting significantly impacts children's emotional development, self-esteem, and interpersonal relationships. Understanding the dynamics and consequences of narcissistic parenting empowers individuals to recognize and address the effects of childhood experiences on their adult lives. By implementing coping strategies and seeking support, adult children of narcissistic parents can cultivate resilience, heal from emotional wounds, and foster healthier relationships and self-concepts. In the subsequent chapters, we will explore interventions and therapeutic approaches aimed at supporting individuals affected by narcissistic parenting and promoting healing and growth.

4.4 Strategies for Coping and Setting Boundaries

Navigating relationships with narcissistic individuals, whether as a partner, child, or family member, requires adaptive strategies for maintaining emotional well-being and asserting personal boundaries.

This section explores effective coping strategies and boundary-setting techniques to manage interactions with narcissistic individuals.

Coping Strategies

1. Recognize Patterns and Behaviors:

Developing awareness of narcissistic traits and behaviors can help you anticipate and navigate interactions more effectively. Understanding typical patterns of manipulation, gaslighting, or emotional volatility empowers you to respond strategically.

2. Practice Self-Care:

Prioritize self-care activities that promote emotional resilience and well-being. Engage in hobbies, exercise, mindfulness practices, or activities that bring joy and relaxation, reducing the emotional impact of interactions with narcissistic individuals.

3. Seek Support:

Build a support network of friends, family members, or a therapist who can provide validation, empathy, and perspective. Discussing your experiences with trusted individuals can offer emotional support and strategies for coping with challenging interactions.

4. Set Realistic Expectations:

Adjust your expectations regarding the narcissistic individual's behavior and reactions. Recognize that you cannot change their personality or motivations, focusing instead on managing your responses and setting boundaries to protect yourself.

Setting Boundaries

1. Define Clear Boundaries:

Identify your boundaries regarding emotional, physical, and social interactions with the narcissistic individual. Clearly articulate your limits and communicate them assertively, reinforcing your right to respect and autonomy.

2. Communicate Assertively:

Use assertive communication techniques to express your boundaries confidently and respectfully. Avoid justifying or defending your boundaries excessively, maintaining a firm and consistent stance.

3. Enforce Consequences:

Establish consequences for boundary violations and communicate them. Consistently follow through with consequences when boundaries are disregarded, reinforcing the importance of respecting your limits.

4. Limit Exposure:

Manage your exposure to the narcissistic individual by setting limits on time spent together or the depth of personal information shared. Create physical or emotional distance when necessary to minimize stress and maintain emotional balance.

Strategies for Specific Relationships

1. Romantic Relationships:

In romantic relationships with narcissistic partners, prioritize self-care, maintain supportive relationships outside the relationship, and consider seeking couples therapy or individual counseling to address relational dynamics.

2. Parental Relationships:

Adult children of narcissistic parents can benefit from setting boundaries, seeking therapy to process childhood experiences, and establishing a support network to navigate ongoing interactions with their parents.

3. Workplace Relationships:

In professional settings, maintain professionalism, document interactions when necessary, and seek guidance from HR or supervisors if behaviors become problematic. Focus on assertive communication and self-care to manage stress.

Long-Term Strategies

1. Emotional Resilience Building:

Invest in activities and practices that strengthen emotional resilience, such as mindfulness meditation, journaling, or engaging in hobbies that promote self-expression and relaxation.

2. Therapeutic Support:

Consider individual therapy to explore and address the emotional impact of relationships with narcissistic individuals. Therapists can provide tools for emotional regulation, boundary-setting, and navigating complex interpersonal dynamics.

3. Personal Growth and Reflection:

Engage in ongoing self-reflection and personal growth activities to understand patterns of interaction and prioritize your own needs and values in relationships. Continuous learning and self-awareness foster healthier relational patterns.

Coping with narcissistic individuals requires intentional strategies for maintaining emotional well-being, setting boundaries, and navigating complex interpersonal dynamics. By prioritizing self-care, seeking support, and assertively communicating boundaries, individuals can mitigate the emotional impact of interactions and cultivate healthier relationships. Implementing these strategies fosters resilience, promotes personal growth, and supports long-term emotional health in relationships affected by narcissistic traits. In the subsequent chapters, we will explore additional interventions and therapeutic approaches aimed at promoting healing, growth, and relational satisfaction in the context of narcissistic relationships.

Chapter 5: Narcissism in the Workplace

Narcissism in the workplace presents complex dynamics that can significantly influence organizational culture, employee interactions, and overall productivity. Understanding how narcissistic behavior manifests and its implications is crucial for fostering a healthy work environment and mitigating potential challenges.

Characteristics of Narcissistic Behavior

In the workplace, narcissistic behavior often manifests in several distinctive ways:

1. Grandiosity and Self-Importance:

Narcissistic individuals often exhibit an exaggerated sense of self-importance and superiority. They may believe they are uniquely talented or deserving of special treatment, seeking admiration and recognition from colleagues and superiors.

2. Lack of Empathy and Emotional Intelligence:

Empathy deficits are common among narcissistic individuals, making it challenging for them to understand or prioritize the emotions and needs of others. This can lead to interpersonal conflicts, as colleagues may feel disregarded or undervalued.

3. Manipulative Tactics:

Narcissists may employ manipulative tactics to achieve personal goals or maintain control over others. This can include using charm, flattery, or intimidation to influence decisions, gain advantages, or undermine perceived rivals.

4. Boundary Violations and Exploitation:

They may disregard professional boundaries, exploit relationships for personal gain, or manipulate situations to suit their agenda. This can create a sense of distrust and instability within teams.

Impact on Organizational Culture

Narcissistic behavior can significantly impact organizational culture:

1. Toxic Work Environment:

In extreme cases, narcissistic behavior can contribute to a toxic work environment characterized by fear, competition, and mistrust. This can erode morale, increase turnover rates, and hinder collaboration and innovation.

2. Leadership Dynamics:

Narcissistic leaders may prioritize their interests over organizational goals, leading to decision-making that favors personal gain or reputation enhancement. This can undermine team cohesion and long-term strategic planning.

3. Conflict and Turbulence:

Their tendency towards conflict and confrontation can create disruptions within teams, leading to power struggles, cliques, or factions that detract from productivity and morale.

Strategies for Managing Narcissism in the Workplace

1. Leadership Awareness and Training:

Educating leaders and managers about narcissistic behavior and its impact is crucial. Providing training on emotional intelligence, conflict resolution, and ethical leadership can help mitigate the negative effects of narcissistic leadership styles.

2. Establishing Clear Policies and Procedures:

Implementing transparent policies regarding communication, performance evaluation, and conflict resolution can provide a framework for addressing and managing narcissistic behavior effectively.

3. Promoting a Culture of Feedback and Accountability:

Encouraging open communication, constructive feedback, and accountability can mitigate the effects of narcissistic behavior by promoting transparency and fairness within the organization.

Managing Interactions with Narcissistic Colleagues

1. Setting and Enforcing Boundaries:

Clearly defining and asserting personal boundaries in professional interactions with narcissistic colleagues is essential. This involves communicating expectations firmly and consistently.

2. Maintaining Professionalism and Composure:

Responding to narcissistic behavior with professionalism and emotional composure can prevent escalations and maintain focus on productive outcomes.

3. Documenting Interactions:

Keeping records of important interactions, emails, and decisions can provide documentation in case of disputes or conflicts involving narcissistic colleagues.

Navigating narcissism in the workplace requires a balanced approach that prioritizes organizational health, employee well-being, and productivity. By understanding the dynamics of narcissistic behavior, implementing strategic interventions, and fostering a supportive work environment, organizations can mitigate challenges and promote a culture of respect, collaboration, and professional growth. In the subsequent chapters, we will explore practical case studies, interventions, and real-world strategies for addressing and managing narcissistic behavior in specific workplace contexts.

5.1 Narcissistic Leadership: Traits and Consequences

Narcissistic leadership is characterized by a constellation of traits and behaviors that can profoundly impact organizational dynamics, employee morale, and overall performance. Leaders with narcissistic traits often exhibit grandiosity, entitlement, a need for admiration, and a lack of empathy. These characteristics can lead to both positive and negative outcomes within the workplace, shaping the organization's culture and functioning in complex ways.

Narcissistic leaders often possess a heightened sense of self-importance and grandiosity. They tend to believe they are uniquely talented and capable, deserving of special treatment and recognition. This grandiosity can manifest in a charismatic and confident leadership style that initially attracts admiration and loyalty from employees. Their vision and confidence can inspire teams, drive ambitious projects, and foster a culture of high performance. However, this same grandiosity can lead to unrealistic expectations, as narcissistic leaders may overestimate their capabilities and the capabilities of their teams, setting unattainable goals and pressuring employees to achieve them.

Entitlement is another hallmark of narcissistic leadership. These leaders often expect to receive preferential treatment and may become frustrated or angry when their perceived entitlements are not met. This sense of entitlement can create an environment where rules and norms are bent or broken to accommodate the leader's desires. It can undermine fairness and equity within the organization, leading to resentment and decreased morale among employees who feel they are held to different standards.

A significant consequence of narcissistic leadership is the impact on employee well-being and engagement. Narcissistic leaders typically lack empathy, making it difficult for them to understand or respond to the emotional needs of their employees. They may dismiss or trivialize the concerns of their team members, focusing instead on their own needs and objectives. This lack of empathy can lead to a toxic work environment where employees feel undervalued, unsupported, and emotionally drained. High levels of stress and burnout are common in such settings, as employees struggle to meet the demands of a leader who offers little emotional support or recognition.

Narcissistic leaders also tend to engage in manipulative behaviors to maintain control and achieve their goals. They may use charm, flattery, and charisma to win over colleagues and subordinates, only to turn to intimidation, bullying, or undermining tactics when faced with opposition or criticism. This manipulative behavior can create a culture of fear and mistrust, where employees are reluctant to speak up, share ideas, or report issues. The resulting lack of open communication can stifle innovation and hinder problem-solving, ultimately impacting the organization's ability to adapt and thrive.

The long-term consequences of narcissistic leadership can be detrimental to organizational health. While the initial charisma and vision of a narcissistic leader may drive short-term successes, the underlying issues of unrealistic expectations, entitlement, lack of empathy, and manipulative behaviors can lead to high employee turnover, decreased job satisfaction, and toxic work culture. Over time, these negative outcomes can erode the organization's reputation, reduce its ability to attract and retain top talent and impact overall performance and profitability.

In conclusion, narcissistic leadership presents a paradox of potential short-term gains overshadowed by significant long-term risks. The grandiosity and confidence of narcissistic leaders can inspire and drive performance, but their entitlement, lack of empathy, and manipulative behaviors can create a toxic work environment, undermine employee well-being, and hinder organizational success. Recognizing and addressing the traits and consequences of narcissistic leadership is crucial for fostering a healthy, supportive, and high-performing workplace.

5.2 Managing Narcissistic Employees and Colleagues

Managing narcissistic employees and colleagues requires a nuanced approach that balances empathy and assertiveness to mitigate the disruptive impact of their behavior while maintaining a productive work environment. Narcissistic individuals in the workplace often exhibit traits such as grandiosity, a need for admiration, a sense of entitlement, and a lack of empathy. These characteristics can lead to conflicts, decreased morale, and a toxic work culture if not managed effectively.

One of the first steps in managing narcissistic employees and colleagues is to recognize and understand their behavior. Narcissistic individuals often seek constant validation and admiration. They may exaggerate their accomplishments and capabilities to appear superior. While their confidence and ambition can drive high performance, these traits can also lead to unrealistic expectations and pressure on their peers. It is essential to approach these individuals with a clear understanding of their need for recognition and to provide constructive feedback that acknowledges their contributions while setting realistic performance expectations.

Establishing clear boundaries is crucial when dealing with narcissistic employees. These individuals may try to test or push limits to get their way or assert dominance. Managers and colleagues must consistently enforce professional boundaries and standards of behavior. This includes setting clear expectations for performance, communication, and conduct, and ensuring that these standards are applied uniformly across the team. By maintaining consistency, managers can prevent narcissistic individuals from exploiting perceived weaknesses or favoritism within the organization.

Effective communication is another key strategy in managing narcissistic colleagues. Narcissistic individuals may engage in manipulative or confrontational tactics to achieve their goals. It is essential to communicate with them in a direct, assertive, and respectful manner. Avoiding emotional reactivity and maintaining professionalism can help prevent the escalation of conflicts. When providing feedback, focus on specific behaviors and their impact on the team or organization, rather than making personal criticisms. This approach can help narcissistic individuals understand the consequences of their actions without feeling personally attacked, which can reduce defensiveness and promote constructive dialogue.

Providing opportunities for narcissistic employees to channel their ambition and need for recognition in positive ways can also be beneficial. Assigning them to high-visibility projects or leadership roles where their contributions can be acknowledged can satisfy their need for admiration while leveraging their strengths for the benefit of the organization. However, it is important to balance these opportunities with accountability to ensure that their behavior aligns with organizational values and goals.

Supporting the well-being of other team members is equally important when managing narcissistic colleagues. The presence of a narcissistic individual can create a challenging work environment for others, leading to stress, frustration, and decreased morale. Providing a supportive environment where employees feel valued and heard can mitigate these negative effects. Encouraging open communication, fostering a culture of respect and inclusivity, and offering resources such as employee assistance programs or conflict resolution training can help support the overall well-being of the team.

In cases where narcissistic behavior becomes particularly disruptive or harmful, more direct intervention may be necessary. This can include formal performance reviews, disciplinary actions, or even termination if the behavior violates organizational policies or significantly impacts team dynamics. It is important to document incidents of problematic behavior and follow established procedures to ensure that actions taken are fair, transparent, and legally compliant.

In conclusion, managing narcissistic employees and colleagues requires a multifaceted approach that includes understanding their behavior, setting clear boundaries, maintaining effective communication, and providing supportive resources for the entire team. By balancing empathy with assertiveness, managers can mitigate the negative impact of narcissistic behavior, foster a positive work environment, and promote a culture of accountability and respect. Implementing these strategies can help organizations navigate the challenges posed by narcissistic individuals and maintain a healthy, productive workplace.

5.3 The Impact on Organizational Culture and Productivity

The presence of narcissistic individuals in the workplace can have profound and multifaceted impacts on organizational culture and productivity. Narcissistic traits such as grandiosity, entitlement, and lack of empathy can influence team dynamics, employee morale, and overall organizational performance in both overt and subtle ways.

Narcissistic leaders and employees often create a work environment characterized by tension and instability. Their need for constant validation and superiority can lead to a culture of competition rather than collaboration. Narcissistic leaders may promote a winner-takes-all mentality, where success is measured by outshining peers rather than working together towards common goals. This competitive atmosphere can stifle teamwork, as employees focus more on individual achievements to gain favor with the narcissistic leader, thereby undermining the spirit of cooperation and mutual support.

One of the most significant impacts of narcissism on organizational culture is the erosion of trust. Narcissistic individuals may engage in manipulative and self-serving behaviors, such as taking credit for others' work, spreading misinformation, or undermining colleagues to maintain their status. These actions can create an environment of suspicion and mistrust, where employees feel insecure and guarded. When trust is compromised, open communication and honest feedback become rare, leading to a lack of transparency and reduced organizational cohesion.

Employee morale is another area heavily affected by the presence of narcissism in the workplace. Narcissistic leaders and colleagues often fail to recognize or appreciate the contributions of others, leading to feelings of undervaluation and resentment. Their tendency to criticize or belittle others can result in a toxic work environment where employees feel demoralized and disengaged. High levels of stress and burnout are common in such environments, as employees struggle to meet unrealistic expectations or cope with constant scrutiny and criticism.

The impact of narcissism extends to organizational productivity. The self-centered focus of narcissistic individuals can divert attention and resources away from collective goals. For instance, a narcissistic leader might prioritize projects that enhance their image or career prospects, rather than those that are strategically important for the organization. This misalignment of priorities can lead to inefficient use of resources and missed opportunities for growth and innovation.

Moreover, the high turnover rates often associated with narcissistic workplaces can further hinder productivity. Talented employees may choose to leave an organization where they feel undervalued or mistreated, resulting in a loss of skills and institutional knowledge. The constant churn of staff can disrupt workflows, increase recruitment and training costs, and reduce overall efficiency.

Narcissistic behavior also impacts decision-making processes within the organization. Narcissistic leaders may dismiss or ignore input from others, believing their judgment to be superior. This can lead to poor decision-making, as critical perspectives and expertise are overlooked. Additionally, fear of retribution may prevent employees from voicing concerns or alternative ideas, further impairing the quality of decisions and innovation.

To mitigate these negative impacts, organizations need to implement strategies that promote a healthy and inclusive culture. Encouraging open communication, fostering a culture of mutual respect, and ensuring fair and transparent recognition and reward systems are essential. Leadership development programs that emphasize emotional intelligence, empathy, and ethical behavior can help counterbalance the influence of narcissistic traits.

Providing support resources for employees, such as counseling services, conflict resolution training, and opportunities for professional development, can also enhance resilience and well-being. Establishing clear policies and procedures for addressing toxic behavior and ensuring consistent enforcement can help maintain a respectful and supportive work environment.

In conclusion, narcissistic individuals can significantly disrupt organizational culture and productivity through their self-centered behaviors and the resulting erosion of trust, morale, and collaboration. By recognizing these impacts and proactively implementing strategies to foster a positive and inclusive culture, organizations can mitigate the detrimental effects of narcissism and promote a healthier, more productive work environment.

5.4 Strategies for Navigating Workplace Narcissism

Navigating workplace narcissism requires a multifaceted approach that combines personal resilience, strategic communication, and organizational policies designed to mitigate the negative impact of narcissistic behavior. Employees and managers alike must be equipped with practical strategies to handle the challenges posed by narcissistic colleagues or leaders.

Understanding the behavior and mindset of narcissistic individuals is the first step in developing effective strategies. Narcissists often exhibit a strong need for admiration, a sense of entitlement, and a lack of empathy. Recognizing these traits can help in predicting their actions and preparing for interactions. When dealing with a narcissistic colleague, it is crucial to maintain a calm and composed demeanor. Emotional reactivity can fuel their behavior, while a steady and professional approach can help in managing conflicts.

Setting clear boundaries is essential when interacting with narcissistic individuals. They may attempt to push limits or exploit situations to their advantage. By defining and consistently enforcing personal and professional boundaries, employees can protect themselves from manipulative tactics. For example, if a narcissistic colleague frequently tries to offload tasks or take credit for others' work, it is important to communicate assertively about responsibilities and expectations. Documenting interactions and agreements can also provide a clear record in case of disputes.

Effective communication is a cornerstone of managing narcissistic behavior. It is important to be direct, concise, and factual when dealing with narcissistic individuals. Avoid engaging in arguments or attempting to outshine them, as this can escalate conflicts. Instead, focus on constructive dialogue that centers on work-related issues and outcomes. When providing feedback, emphasize specific behaviors and their impact on the team or project, rather than making personal criticisms. This approach can help reduce defensiveness and promote a more productive conversation.

In addition to personal strategies, organizational policies play a crucial role in navigating workplace narcissism. Implementing clear policies on communication, performance evaluations, and conflict resolution can provide a framework for addressing narcissistic behavior. These policies should emphasize fairness, transparency, and accountability, ensuring that all employees are held to the same standards. Regular training sessions on emotional intelligence, leadership, and conflict management can equip employees and managers with the skills needed to handle difficult interactions.

Creating a supportive work environment is also vital. Providing resources such as employee assistance programs, counseling services, and professional development opportunities can help employees cope with the stress associated with working with narcissistic individuals. Encouraging open communication and a culture of mutual respect can mitigate the impact of narcissistic behavior on team dynamics. Regular check-ins and team-building activities can foster a sense of community and support among employees, making it easier to navigate challenges collectively.

Leadership development programs that emphasize ethical behavior, empathy, and emotional intelligence can help prevent the rise of narcissistic leaders. By promoting a culture of servant leadership, where leaders prioritize the well-being and development of their teams, organizations can counterbalance the influence of narcissism. Mentorship programs can also provide guidance and support for emerging leaders, helping them develop a balanced and inclusive approach to leadership.

In some cases, more direct intervention may be necessary. If narcissistic behavior becomes particularly disruptive or harmful, formal performance reviews, disciplinary actions, or even termination may be required. It is important to follow established procedures and document all actions taken to ensure fairness and compliance with organizational policies and legal requirements.

In conclusion, navigating workplace narcissism involves a combination of personal resilience, strategic communication, and organizational policies that promote a healthy and inclusive culture. By understanding narcissistic behavior, setting clear boundaries, maintaining effective communication, and fostering a supportive environment, employees and managers can mitigate the negative impact of narcissism and promote a more productive and harmonious workplace. Implementing these strategies requires a concerted effort from individuals and organizations alike, but the benefits of a healthier work environment are well worth the investment.

Chapter 6: Self-Identity and Narcissism

Narcissism profoundly impacts self-identity, shaping how individuals perceive themselves and interact with the world. This chapter explores the intricate relationship between self-identity and narcissism, examining the psychological underpinnings, the role of self-perception, and how narcissistic traits influence personal and social identities.

1. The Narcissistic Self-Concept

The core of narcissism lies in an inflated self-concept. Narcissistic individuals often view themselves as superior, unique, and deserving of special treatment. This grandiose self-concept is typically a defense mechanism to protect against deep-seated feelings of inadequacy and vulnerability. The narcissistic self is constructed on the need for admiration and validation from others. Consequently, narcissists invest heavily in maintaining an idealized image, often at the expense of authentic self-awareness and personal growth.

This inflated self-concept can be traced back to early developmental experiences. Narcissistic individuals may have received excessive praise or criticism during childhood, leading to an unstable self-image. The constant need for external validation stems from a lack of internal self-worth, driving the narcissist to seek approval and admiration continuously. This external focus makes it challenging for narcissists to engage in genuine self-reflection and develop a stable, realistic sense of self.

2. Self-Perception and Narcissistic Traits

Self-perception in narcissistic individuals is often marked by dichotomous thinking, where they view themselves in extremes of either greatness or worthlessness. This black-and-white thinking can lead to fluctuating self-esteem, heavily influenced by external feedback. Positive reinforcement can temporarily boost their self-esteem, while criticism or failure can trigger feelings of worthlessness and intense defensiveness.

Narcissistic traits such as grandiosity, entitlement, and lack of empathy shape how individuals perceive themselves and their relationships with others. Grandiosity leads to an exaggerated sense of one's abilities and achievements, fostering unrealistic self-perceptions. Entitlement creates a belief that one deserves special privileges, often resulting in frustration and resentment when these expectations are not met. Lack of empathy hinders the ability to understand and connect with others, reinforcing a self-centered worldview that prioritizes one's needs and desires above all else.

3. The Impact on Social Identity

Narcissism significantly influences social identity, affecting how individuals interact with their social environment and construct their roles within it. Narcissistic individuals often prioritize relationships that enhance their self-image and provide validation. They may associate with people who reinforce their grandiose self-perceptions while avoiding or devaluing those who challenge them.

This selective engagement can lead to superficial relationships, as narcissists focus more on the image they project rather than genuine connections. Their social identity is often built around roles that offer prestige, power, or admiration. In professional settings, this can manifest as a relentless pursuit of status and recognition, sometimes at the expense of ethical considerations and collaborative efforts.

The need for admiration and validation also drives narcissists to engage in social comparison. They constantly measure themselves against others, striving to outshine and outperform their peers. This competitive nature can foster envy and resentment, further complicating their social interactions and perpetuating a cycle of superficial connections and dissatisfaction.

4. Challenges to Authentic Self-Identity

The pursuit of an idealized self-image and the reliance on external validation pose significant challenges to the development of an authentic self-identity in narcissistic individuals. The focus on maintaining a façade prevents genuine self-exploration and acceptance of one's strengths and weaknesses. Narcissists may struggle to reconcile their public persona with their private self, leading to inner conflict and a fragmented sense of identity.

Moreover, the lack of empathy and genuine emotional connection with others can hinder personal growth and self-awareness. Narcissistic individuals may find it difficult to engage in meaningful introspection or accept constructive criticism, impeding their ability to develop a well-rounded and realistic self-concept.

5. Pathways to Self-Reflection and Growth

Despite these challenges, narcissistic individuals can cultivate a more authentic self-identity through self-reflection and personal growth. This process often requires therapeutic intervention to help individuals confront and understand their deep-seated insecurities and vulnerabilities. Therapy can provide a safe space for narcissists to explore their self-perceptions, challenge their unrealistic beliefs, and develop healthier coping mechanisms.

Encouraging self-awareness and empathy is crucial in this journey. Mindfulness practices, journaling, and other reflective activities can help narcissistic individuals connect with their inner selves and develop a more balanced and authentic self-identity. Building genuine relationships based on mutual respect and understanding can also foster emotional growth and a deeper sense of connection with others.

Narcissism profoundly shapes self-identity, influencing how individuals perceive themselves and interact with the world. The inflated self-concept and reliance on external validation can lead to a fragmented and unstable sense of self. By understanding the psychological underpinnings of narcissistic traits and their impact on self-perception and social identity, individuals and therapists can work towards fostering self-reflection, authenticity, and personal growth. In the following chapters, we will explore therapeutic approaches and strategies for supporting narcissistic individuals in their journey toward a healthier and more integrated self-identity.

6.1 The Narcissistic Self-Concept

The narcissistic self-concept is characterized by an inflated sense of self-importance and an incessant need for admiration. At its core, this self-concept is built on grandiosity and an idealized image of oneself, often as a defense mechanism against deep-seated feelings of inadequacy and low self-esteem. Understanding the narcissistic self-concept involves exploring the psychological foundations of these traits and their manifestations in daily life.

Narcissistic individuals view themselves as exceptional and superior to others. They believe they possess unique qualities that set them apart, deserving special treatment and recognition. This grandiose self-image is not just about thinking highly of oneself; it is an exaggerated and unrealistic perception that goes beyond normal self-confidence. Narcissists often fantasize about unlimited success, power, brilliance, beauty, or ideal love, which fuels their sense of entitlement and expectation of preferential treatment.

The narcissistic self-concept is largely contingent on external validation. Narcissistic individuals seek constant reinforcement of their self-worth from others. They crave admiration, praise, and recognition to sustain their grandiose self-image. When they receive this validation, their self-esteem temporarily soars. However, this self-esteem is fragile and heavily dependent on others' perceptions. Any form of criticism, rejection, or perceived slight can lead to a rapid decline in self-esteem, triggering defensive behaviors to protect their inflated self-view.

The development of the narcissistic self-concept can often be traced back to early childhood experiences. Two primary pathways are commonly cited: excessive pampering and excessive criticism. In cases of excessive pampering, children may be overvalued by their parents, receiving constant praise and admiration that instills an inflated sense of self-importance. These children learn to expect and demand this level of attention and validation from others as they grow older.

On the other hand, excessive criticism or neglect can also contribute to the development of narcissism. Children who experience significant criticism or emotional neglect may develop an inflated self-concept as a defense mechanism to protect themselves from feelings of worthlessness and inadequacy. By creating an idealized image of themselves, they attempt to shield their fragile self-esteem from further harm.

The narcissistic self-concept is also marked by a lack of genuine self-awareness. Narcissistic individuals struggle to engage in honest self-reflection and to acknowledge their flaws and limitations. They often use defense mechanisms such as denial, projection, and rationalization to maintain their grandiose self-image. For instance, they might blame others for their failures or shortcomings, rather than accepting personal responsibility. This lack of self-awareness hinders personal growth and the development of a realistic and integrated self-concept.

In social interactions, the narcissistic self-concept manifests as a need to dominate and control. Narcissistic individuals often seek positions of power and authority where they can receive the admiration and attention they crave. They may exploit relationships to boost their self-esteem, using others as a means to reinforce their grandiosity. However, their lack of empathy and genuine emotional connection can lead to superficial relationships that lack depth and authenticity.

The constant pursuit of validation can also lead to feelings of envy and resentment. Narcissistic individuals may compare themselves to others, feeling threatened by those who appear more successful or competent. This competitive nature can drive them to undermine or devalue others to protect their self-image.

In conclusion, the narcissistic self-concept is a complex interplay of grandiosity, dependency on external validation, and defense mechanisms to protect fragile self-esteem. This inflated self-image, rooted in early developmental experiences, shapes how narcissistic individuals perceive themselves and interact with the world. Understanding the narcissistic self-concept is crucial for developing therapeutic approaches to help narcissistic individuals achieve a more realistic and integrated sense of self.

6.2 Self-Esteem and Narcissistic Insecurity

Narcissistic individuals present a paradoxical blend of high self-esteem and deep-seated insecurity. On the surface, they appear confident and self-assured, but beneath this veneer lies a fragile sense of self-worth that is highly dependent on external validation. This section delves into the intricate relationship between self-esteem and narcissistic insecurity, exploring how these dynamics manifest and affect behavior.

The Facade of High Self-Esteem

At first glance, narcissistic individuals often exhibit high self-esteem. They project an image of confidence, superiority, and unwavering self-assurance. This grandiose self-esteem is typically characterized by an exaggerated sense of one's abilities, achievements, and importance. Narcissists frequently engage in self-promotion, boast about their accomplishments, and seek admiration from others. Their outward demeanor suggests a robust and unshakeable self-worth.

This high self-esteem, however, is largely superficial. It is not rooted in a realistic self-assessment or a stable sense of inner worth. Instead, it is a facade constructed to mask underlying insecurities. Narcissists' grandiose self-esteem is highly contingent on external reinforcement;

they rely on constant praise, attention, and validation to sustain their inflated self-image. Without this external affirmation, their self-esteem quickly diminishes, exposing their underlying insecurity.

The Fragility of Narcissistic Insecurity

Despite their outward confidence, narcissistic individuals are often plagued by profound insecurity. Their grandiose self-esteem is a defensive mechanism designed to protect against feelings of inadequacy and vulnerability. This insecurity stems from a deeply ingrained fear of being exposed as flawed, unworthy, or inferior. As a result, narcissists are hypersensitive to criticism, rejection, and failure.

When faced with criticism or perceived slights, narcissists react defensively. They may respond with anger, denial, or attempts to discredit the source of criticism. These reactions are efforts to protect their fragile self-esteem and avoid confronting their insecurities. The defensive behaviors are often disproportionate to the actual threat, highlighting the underlying vulnerability they are trying to conceal.

The Role of External Validation

External validation plays a crucial role in the dynamics of narcissistic self-esteem and insecurity. Narcissists crave admiration and approval from others to maintain their grandiose self-image. Positive feedback temporarily boosts their self-esteem, reinforcing their belief in their superiority. However, this boost is fleeting, and narcissists require continuous validation to keep their insecurities at bay.

The dependency on external validation creates a precarious situation. Narcissistic individuals are constantly seeking new sources of admiration, which can lead to manipulative or exploitative behaviors. They may surround themselves with people who reinforce their self-image and avoid those who challenge it. This reliance on external validation prevents them from developing a stable and authentic sense of self-worth.

Coping Mechanisms and Defense Strategies

To manage their insecurities, narcissists employ various coping mechanisms and defense strategies. These include denial, projection, and rationalization. For instance, a narcissist might deny any personal responsibility for failure, instead blaming external factors or other people. Projection involves attributing their flaws and insecurities to others, while rationalization provides seemingly logical explanations for their behavior, even when it is self-serving or harmful.

These defense mechanisms protect the narcissist's self-esteem but also hinder self-awareness and personal growth. By avoiding introspection and externalizing blame, narcissistic individuals prevent themselves from addressing the root causes of their insecurities. This perpetuates a cycle of dependence on external validation and defensive behavior.

The Impact on Relationships and Work

The interplay between self-esteem and insecurity in narcissistic individuals has significant implications for their relationships and professional life. In relationships, their need for admiration can lead to exploitative dynamics, where partners are valued primarily for the validation they provide. This can result in superficial connections that lack genuine emotional intimacy.

In the workplace, narcissistic insecurity can manifest as a relentless pursuit of recognition and success. Narcissists may engage in competitive or manipulative behaviors to maintain their self-esteem, often at the expense of colleagues or organizational goals. Their hypersensitivity to criticism can create a challenging work environment, where constructive feedback is met with defensiveness and hostility.

Towards Authentic Self-Esteem

Addressing the fragile self-esteem and underlying insecurity of narcissistic individuals requires a shift toward developing authentic self-worth. This involves moving away from reliance on external validation and fostering genuine self-awareness and acceptance. Therapeutic interventions can help narcissists explore their insecurities, challenge their defense mechanisms, and build a more stable and realistic sense of self-esteem.

Encouraging self-reflection, empathy, and emotional intelligence can also promote personal growth. By learning to value themselves independently of external validation and understanding the impact of their behavior on others, narcissistic individuals can develop healthier self-esteem and more meaningful relationships.

The relationship between self-esteem and narcissistic insecurity is complex and multifaceted. While narcissists project high self-esteem, it is often a fragile facade that conceals deep-seated insecurities. Their reliance on external validation and defensive behaviors underscores the vulnerability of their self-worth. Understanding these dynamics is crucial for developing effective therapeutic approaches and fostering healthier, more authentic self-esteem in narcissistic individuals.

6.3 The Role of Social Media and Modern Culture

Social media and modern culture play a significant role in shaping and reinforcing narcissistic traits and behaviors. The rise of platforms such as Instagram, Facebook, and Twitter has created an environment where self-promotion, image management, and the pursuit of external validation are not only commonplace but often encouraged. This section explores how social media and contemporary cultural norms influence narcissism, amplify narcissistic tendencies, and affect individuals' self-perception and behavior.

Social Media: A Catalyst for Narcissism

Social media platforms provide a stage for individuals to curate and broadcast their lives, often in ways that emphasize the most positive and glamorous aspects. This curation fosters a culture of comparison and competition, where users strive to present an idealized version of themselves. For narcissistic individuals, these platforms offer a fertile ground for seeking admiration and validation. The ability to garner "likes," comments, and followers serves as a direct measure of social approval, reinforcing their need for external validation.

The emphasis on visual content, particularly on platforms like Instagram and TikTok, highlights physical appearance and lifestyle, aspects that narcissistic individuals often prioritize. They meticulously craft their online personas to attract attention and admiration, using filters, staged photos, and selective sharing to construct a desirable image. This focus on appearance and status aligns with narcissistic traits of grandiosity and the pursuit of recognition.

Modern Culture: Valuing Appearance and Success

Modern culture, particularly in Western societies, often values individualism, material success, and physical attractiveness. These cultural norms can amplify narcissistic tendencies by promoting values that align with narcissistic traits. The emphasis on personal achievement, wealth, and beauty can drive individuals to adopt behaviors and attitudes that prioritize these aspects, often at the expense of genuine self-awareness and interpersonal relationships.

Reality television, celebrity culture, and influencer lifestyles further reinforce these values. Public figures who exemplify narcissistic traits, such as self-promotion, entitlement, and a focus on external success, are often celebrated and emulated. This cultural backdrop creates a feedback loop where narcissistic behaviors are not only normalized but rewarded, encouraging individuals to adopt similar traits to gain social recognition and status.

The Psychology of Online Behavior

The psychology of online behavior reveals how social media can exacerbate narcissistic tendencies. The anonymity and distance provided by digital interactions reduce the immediate consequences of behavior, allowing individuals to act in ways they might avoid in face-to-face interactions. Narcissists may engage in more aggressive self-promotion, trolling, or cyberbullying, behaviors that stem from their need to dominate and receive attention.

The design of social media platforms also plays a role. Algorithms prioritize content that generates engagement, often favoring sensational or emotionally charged posts. Narcissistic individuals, adept at capturing attention, may thrive in this environment, receiving more visibility and reinforcement for their behavior. This continuous cycle of posting, receiving feedback, and adjusting content to maximize engagement reinforces their need for external validation and can deepen narcissistic traits.

Impact on Self-Identity and Relationships

The interplay between social media, modern culture, and narcissism significantly impacts self-identity and relationships. For many individuals, the constant comparison to idealized representations of others can lead to feelings of inadequacy and diminished self-worth. Narcissistic individuals, while seemingly confident, are particularly vulnerable to these comparisons. Their reliance on external validation makes them sensitive to perceived shortcomings and can exacerbate their insecurities.

In relationships, the emphasis on self-promotion and image management can hinder genuine connections. Narcissistic individuals may prioritize relationships that enhance their social status or provide validation, often at the expense of deeper emotional bonds. This can lead to superficial interactions and difficulties in maintaining long-term, meaningful relationships.

Mitigating the Influence of Social Media and Culture

Addressing the influence of social media and modern culture on narcissism involves both individual and societal efforts. On an individual level, fostering self-awareness and critical thinking about online behavior can help mitigate the impact. Encouraging people to reflect on their motivations for using social media, the authenticity of their online persona, and the effects of comparison can promote healthier interactions and self-perceptions.

From a societal perspective, promoting digital literacy and emotional intelligence can help individuals navigate the complexities of online environments. Education about the psychological effects of social media, the pitfalls of comparison, and the importance of self-compassion can build resilience against the pressures of modern culture. Social media platforms themselves can also play a role by implementing features that promote well-being, such as tools to limit screen time, reduce exposure to harmful content, and encourage positive interactions.

Social media and modern culture significantly influence the development and expression of narcissistic traits. The emphasis on self-promotion, appearance, and external validation in these environments aligns with and amplifies narcissistic tendencies. Understanding the psychological mechanisms at play and their impact on self-identity and relationships is crucial for developing strategies to mitigate these influences. By fostering self-awareness, promoting digital literacy, and encouraging healthier cultural values, individuals and societies can better navigate the challenges posed by social media and modern culture in relation to narcissism.

6.4 The Pursuit of Perfection and External Validation

The pursuit of perfection and the relentless quest for external validation are central to understanding narcissism. These pursuits are driven by deep-seated insecurities and an overwhelming need to maintain an idealized self-image. This section delves into the dynamics of perfectionism and external validation in narcissistic individuals, exploring how these behaviors manifest and impact their lives.

The Allure of Perfection

Perfectionism in narcissistic individuals is often a response to internal feelings of inadequacy and vulnerability. By striving for perfection, narcissists attempt to create and maintain an idealized version of themselves that is invulnerable to criticism and failure. This pursuit is not limited to a single aspect of their lives but encompasses various domains, including appearance, achievements, relationships, and social status.

Narcissists' perfectionism is characterized by unattainably high standards and an obsessive focus on flaws and shortcomings. They often set unrealistic goals and expectations for themselves and others, leading to a perpetual cycle of striving and dissatisfaction. The fear of failure and the potential exposure of their perceived inadequacies drive them to overcompensate through meticulous attention to detail, relentless self-improvement, and avoidance of situations where they might fall short.

External Validation: The Narcissist's Lifeline

External validation is the lifeblood of the narcissistic self-concept. Narcissistic individuals rely heavily on the admiration, approval, and recognition of others to sustain their grandiose self-image. This dependency on external feedback creates a fragile self-esteem that is highly susceptible to fluctuations based on others' perceptions.

The need for external validation drives narcissists to engage in behaviors designed to elicit praise and admiration. They may seek out positions of power, fame, or influence, where they can command attention and accolades. In social interactions, they often dominate conversations, highlight their achievements, and seek to impress others with their perceived superiority. Their social media presence is typically curated to present an idealized image that attracts validation and admiration from a broad audience.

However, this dependency on external validation is a double-edged sword. While positive feedback can temporarily boost their self-esteem, any form of criticism, rejection, or lack of recognition can lead to significant emotional distress. Narcissists may react to such situations with anger, defensiveness, or attempts to discredit the source of the perceived threat. This hypersensitivity to external feedback underscores the underlying insecurity that their grandiose self-image attempts to mask.

The Impact of Perfectionism and Validation-Seeking on Mental Health

The relentless pursuit of perfection and external validation takes a toll on the mental health of narcissistic individuals. The constant striving for unattainable standards can lead to chronic stress, anxiety, and burnout. The fear of failure and the need to maintain an impeccable facade can create immense pressure, resulting in emotional exhaustion and decreased well-being.

Moreover, the reliance on external validation can create a sense of emptiness and lack of fulfillment. Narcissistic individuals may find that the admiration and approval they seek are never enough to fill the void of their insecure self-esteem. This perpetual dissatisfaction can lead to feelings of emptiness, depression, and a persistent sense of inadequacy.

The Interpersonal Costs of Perfectionism and Validation-Seeking

The pursuit of perfection and external validation also has significant interpersonal costs. Narcissistic individuals' unrealistic expectations and critical nature can strain relationships with family, friends, and colleagues. Their need for admiration may lead them to exploit others for validation, resulting in superficial connections that lack genuine emotional depth.

In romantic relationships, narcissists' perfectionism and validation-seeking behaviors can create a dynamic where partners feel constantly judged and undervalued. The narcissist's inability to accept flaws or failures, both in themselves and their partners, can lead to conflict, dissatisfaction, and eventual relationship breakdowns. Their hypersensitivity to criticism and rejection can also result in volatile relationships, where partners feel they must continually cater to the narcissist's need for validation to maintain harmony.

Pathways to Healthier Self-Esteem

Addressing the perfectionism and need for external validation in narcissistic individuals requires a multifaceted approach that fosters self-awareness, self-compassion, and authentic self-esteem. Therapeutic interventions can help narcissists recognize and challenge their unrealistic standards and the underlying insecurities driving their behavior. Cognitive-behavioral therapy (CBT) and other therapeutic modalities can assist in developing healthier thought patterns and coping mechanisms.

Encouraging self-compassion and acceptance of imperfections is crucial for breaking the cycle of perfectionism. Mindfulness practices, self-reflective exercises, and therapy can help narcissistic individuals cultivate a more balanced and realistic self-perception. Building internal sources of validation, such as personal values, achievements, and self-worth, can reduce their dependency on external feedback.

The pursuit of perfection and external validation is central to the narcissistic experience, driven by deep-seated insecurities and the need to maintain an idealized self-image. While these behaviors can temporarily bolster self-esteem, they ultimately lead to chronic dissatisfaction, mental health challenges, and strained relationships. By fostering self-awareness, self-compassion, and healthier sources of validation, narcissistic individuals can work towards developing a more stable and authentic sense of self-worth. This journey requires a commitment to introspection and personal growth, but it offers the potential for a more fulfilling and balanced life.

Chapter 7: Treatment and Management of NPD

The treatment and management of Narcissistic Personality Disorder (NPD) are challenging yet essential for improving the quality of life for those affected by it and for those around them. NPD's pervasive patterns of grandiosity, need for admiration, and lack of empathy can lead to significant interpersonal difficulties, emotional distress, and functional impairment. This chapter explores various therapeutic approaches, management strategies, and practical interventions for addressing NPD.

1. Psychotherapy: The Cornerstone of Treatment

Psychotherapy is the primary mode of treatment for NPD, with several approaches showing promise in addressing the complex psychological issues at play. The therapeutic relationship itself is crucial, as individuals with NPD often struggle with trust and vulnerability. Establishing a strong, empathetic, and non-judgmental therapeutic alliance is fundamental to successful treatment.

Cognitive-behavioral therapy (CBT)

Cognitive-behavioral therapy focuses on identifying and changing maladaptive thought patterns and behaviors. For individuals with NPD, CBT can help challenge distorted beliefs about themselves and others, address unrealistic expectations, and develop healthier coping mechanisms. Techniques such as cognitive restructuring, behavioral experiments, and skills training can be particularly beneficial.

Dialectical Behavior Therapy (DBT)

Originally developed for borderline personality disorder, Dialectical Behavior Therapy has been adapted for NPD to address issues of emotional dysregulation and interpersonal conflict. DBT emphasizes mindfulness, distress tolerance, emotion regulation, and interpersonal effectiveness. These skills can help narcissistic individuals manage intense emotions, reduce impulsive behaviors, and improve their relationships.

Psychodynamic Therapy

Psychodynamic therapy delves into the unconscious processes and early developmental experiences that contribute to the formation of narcissistic traits. This approach seeks to uncover and resolve deep-seated emotional conflicts, helping individuals gain insight into their behaviors and motivations. Through techniques such as free association, dream analysis, and transference, psychodynamic therapy aims to foster self-awareness and emotional growth.

Schema Therapy

Schema Therapy combines elements of CBT, psychodynamic therapy, and attachment theory to address deeply ingrained patterns of thought and behavior, known as schemas. For individuals with NPD, schema therapy targets maladaptive schemas related to entitlement, grandiosity, and vulnerability. By reworking these schemas, clients can develop a more realistic and compassionate self-view.

2. Pharmacotherapy: A Supplementary Approach

While no medications are specifically approved for treating NPD, pharmacotherapy can be useful in managing co-occurring conditions and symptoms, such as depression, anxiety, and impulsivity. Selective serotonin reuptake inhibitors (SSRIs), mood stabilizers, and antipsychotic medications may be prescribed based on individual needs. Medication can help stabilize mood and reduce symptom severity, making psychotherapy more effective.

3. Group Therapy and Support Groups

Group therapy offers a unique setting for individuals with NPD to practice social skills, receive feedback, and develop empathy. In a controlled environment, participants can learn from others' experiences, gain different perspectives, and enhance their interpersonal relationships. Support groups specifically tailored for NPD or personality disorders can provide a sense of community and reduce feelings of isolation.

4. Family Therapy and Education

Family therapy is essential in addressing the impact of NPD on relationships and improving family dynamics. It helps family members understand the disorder, set healthy boundaries, and develop effective communication strategies. Education about NPD can reduce blame, foster empathy, and promote a supportive environment for the individual undergoing treatment.

5. Strategies for Self-Management and Personal Growth

Self-management strategies empower individuals with NPD to take an active role in their recovery and personal development. These strategies include:

- **Mindfulness and Meditation**: Practicing mindfulness and meditation can help individuals with NPD become more aware of their thoughts and emotions, reducing impulsive reactions and promoting emotional regulation.
- **Journaling**: Writing about experiences and feelings can foster self-reflection and insight, helping individuals understand their behaviors and motivations.
- **Goal Setting**: Setting realistic and achievable goals can provide a sense of purpose and accomplishment, counteracting feelings of inadequacy and boosting self-esteem.
- **Developing Empathy**: Engaging in activities that promote empathy, such as volunteering or reading literature that explores diverse perspectives, can enhance understanding and compassion for others.

6. Managing Relapses and Setbacks

Relapses and setbacks are common in the treatment of NPD, given the deeply ingrained nature of narcissistic traits. It's essential to view these occurrences as opportunities for learning and growth rather than failures. Strategies for managing relapses include:

- **Ongoing Therapy**: Continuously engaging in therapy, even during periods of stability, helps reinforce progress and address emerging issues.
- **Support Networks**: Maintaining strong support networks, including family, friends, and support groups, provides a safety net during challenging times.
- **Coping Strategies**: Developing and regularly practicing coping strategies, such as relaxation techniques, healthy lifestyle habits, and stress management, can mitigate the impact of stressors that may trigger relapses.

The treatment and management of Narcissistic Personality Disorder require a comprehensive, multifaceted approach that addresses the psychological, emotional, and social dimensions of the disorder. While challenging, effective treatment can lead to significant improvements in self-awareness, emotional regulation, and interpersonal relationships. By leveraging psychotherapy, pharmacotherapy, group therapy, family involvement, and self-management strategies, individuals with NPD can work towards healthier, more fulfilling lives.

7.1 Therapeutic Approaches: Psychotherapy and Counseling

Psychotherapy and counseling form the cornerstone of treating Narcissistic Personality Disorder (NPD). These approaches aim to address the underlying psychological issues, promote self-awareness, and foster healthier interpersonal behaviors. Various therapeutic modalities have been developed and adapted to meet the specific needs of individuals with NPD. This section explores the key therapeutic approaches used in treating NPD, highlighting their principles, techniques, and efficacy.

Cognitive-behavioral therapy (CBT)

Cognitive-behavioral therapy (CBT) is a widely used approach that focuses on identifying and modifying dysfunctional thoughts, beliefs, and behaviors. For individuals with NPD, CBT can be particularly effective in challenging grandiose thinking, entitlement, and the need for admiration. The core techniques of CBT include cognitive restructuring, behavioral experiments, and skills training.

- **Cognitive Restructuring**: This involves identifying and challenging distorted beliefs and cognitive distortions. For example, a narcissistic individual might hold the belief that they are superior to others and deserve special treatment. Cognitive restructuring helps them recognize these beliefs as unrealistic and develop more balanced, realistic thoughts.
- **Behavioral Experiments**: These are practical exercises designed to test the validity of distorted beliefs. For instance, a narcissist who believes they must always appear perfect might be encouraged to engage in an activity where they risk making a mistake, observing that the consequences are not as dire as they anticipated.
- **Skills Training**: This aspect of CBT involves teaching practical skills such as emotion regulation, communication, and empathy. These skills are crucial for improving interpersonal relationships and reducing narcissistic behaviors.

Dialectical Behavior Therapy (DBT)

Originally developed for borderline personality disorder, Dialectical Behavior Therapy (DBT) has been adapted for use with NPD. DBT focuses on balancing acceptance and change, helping individuals manage intense emotions and improve interpersonal effectiveness.

- **Mindfulness**: This practice helps individuals become more aware of their thoughts and feelings in the present moment, reducing impulsive behaviors and increasing emotional regulation.
- **Distress Tolerance**: Techniques in this module teach individuals how to cope with and tolerate distressing emotions without resorting to maladaptive behaviors.
- **Emotion Regulation**: DBT provides tools for understanding and managing intense emotions, which is particularly beneficial for narcissistic individuals who often struggle with emotional dysregulation.
- **Interpersonal Effectiveness**: This module focuses on improving communication and relationship skills, helping individuals assert their needs appropriately and develop healthier connections with others.

Psychodynamic Therapy

Psychodynamic therapy explores the unconscious processes and early developmental experiences that contribute to narcissistic traits. This approach aims to uncover and resolve deep-seated emotional conflicts, fostering greater self-awareness and emotional growth.

- **Free Association**: Clients are encouraged to express their thoughts and feelings freely, revealing unconscious conflicts and patterns.

- **Dream Analysis**: Examining the content of dreams can provide insight into unconscious fears and desires that influence narcissistic behavior.
- **Transference**: This technique involves exploring the transfer of feelings and attitudes from significant others in the client's past onto the therapist, which can reveal unresolved issues and patterns of relating.

Schema Therapy

Schema Therapy combines elements of CBT, psychodynamic therapy, and attachment theory to address deeply ingrained patterns of thought and behavior, known as schemas. For individuals with NPD, schema therapy targets maladaptive schemas related to entitlement, grandiosity, and vulnerability.

- **Identifying Schemas**: The first step involves identifying the specific schemas that underlie narcissistic behavior, such as defectiveness/shame or entitlement/grandiosity.
- **Schema Modes**: Understanding different schema modes (states of mind) helps individuals recognize when they are acting out of a maladaptive schema.
- **Reparenting and Limited Reparenting**: These techniques involve the therapist providing a corrective emotional experience, helping clients meet their unmet emotional needs more healthily.

Mentalization-Based Treatment (MBT)

Mentalization-based treatment (MBT) focuses on improving the ability to understand and interpret one's own and others' mental states. This is particularly relevant for individuals with NPD, who often have difficulties with empathy and perspective-taking.

- **Mentalization Exercises**: These exercises help clients practice considering multiple perspectives and understanding the mental states behind their own and others' behaviors.
- **Reflective Functioning**: Enhancing reflective functioning helps individuals better regulate their emotions and respond more adaptively in interpersonal situations.

Psychotherapy and counseling are vital components of the treatment and management of Narcissistic Personality Disorder. Through various therapeutic approaches, individuals with NPD can gain greater self-awareness, challenge maladaptive beliefs and behaviors, and develop healthier ways of relating to themselves and others. By addressing the underlying psychological issues and promoting personal growth, psychotherapy offers a pathway to more balanced and fulfilling lives for those affected by NPD.

7.2 Medications and Their Efficacy

While psychotherapy remains the primary treatment for Narcissistic Personality Disorder (NPD), medications can play a supplementary role in managing co-occurring conditions and specific symptoms. There are no medications specifically approved for NPD itself, but pharmacotherapy can help alleviate associated symptoms such as depression, anxiety, and mood swings. This section explores the types of medications commonly used in treating individuals with NPD, their mechanisms of action, and their efficacy.

Antidepressants

Selective Serotonin Reuptake Inhibitors (SSRIs): SSRIs, such as fluoxetine (Prozac), sertraline (Zoloft), and escitalopram (Lexapro), are often prescribed to manage depressive symptoms and anxiety disorders that commonly co-occur with NPD. These medications work by increasing serotonin levels in the brain, which can help improve mood and reduce anxiety.

- **Efficacy**: SSRIs are generally well-tolerated and have a good safety profile. They can be effective in reducing symptoms of depression and anxiety, thereby improving overall emotional stability. However, their impact on core narcissistic traits is limited.
- **Serotonin-Norepinephrine Reuptake Inhibitors (SNRIs)**: SNRIs, such as venlafaxine (Effexor) and duloxetine (Cymbalta), are another class of antidepressants that can be used to treat co-occurring depressive and anxiety symptoms. They work by increasing the levels of both serotonin and norepinephrine in the brain.
- **Efficacy**: SNRIs can be effective for individuals who do not respond well to SSRIs. They help manage mood and anxiety symptoms but, similar to SSRIs, do not directly address the core features of NPD.

Mood Stabilizers

- **Lithium**: Lithium is a mood stabilizer commonly used to treat bipolar disorder, but it can also be helpful for individuals with NPD who experience severe mood swings or impulsive behaviors.
- **Efficacy**: Lithium has been shown to stabilize mood and reduce impulsivity. However, it requires regular monitoring due to potential side effects, such as thyroid and kidney issues.
- **Anticonvulsants**: Medications such as valproate (Depakote) and lamotrigine (Lamictal) are also used as mood stabilizers. They can help manage mood fluctuations and impulsive behaviors associated with NPD.
- **Efficacy**: Anticonvulsants can be effective in stabilizing mood and reducing aggression and impulsivity. They are often used as an alternative to lithium for individuals who cannot tolerate its side effects.

Antipsychotics

- **Atypical Antipsychotics**: Medications such as risperidone (Risperdal), olanzapine (Zyprexa), and aripiprazole (Abilify) are used to treat severe mood disturbances, aggression, and impulsivity in individuals with NPD. These medications work by modulating dopamine and serotonin levels in the brain.
- **Efficacy**: Atypical antipsychotics can be effective in reducing irritability, aggression, and severe mood symptoms. They are often used in conjunction with other treatments for individuals with significant behavioral disturbances.

Anti-Anxiety Medications

- **Benzodiazepines**: Medications such as alprazolam (Xanax), diazepam (Valium), and lorazepam (Ativan) are used to manage acute anxiety symptoms. However, due to their potential for dependence and abuse, they are typically prescribed for short-term use.
- **Efficacy**: Benzodiazepines can provide rapid relief from acute anxiety and panic symptoms. However, they are not suitable for long-term management due to the risk of dependency and the potential for exacerbating impulsive behaviors.
- **Buspirone (Buspar)**: Buspirone is an anti-anxiety medication that is less likely to cause dependence compared to benzodiazepines. It works by affecting serotonin and dopamine receptors in the brain.
- **Efficacy**: Buspirone is effective for managing generalized anxiety and has a lower risk of dependence. However, it may take several weeks to achieve its full therapeutic effect.

Considerations and Monitoring

When using medications to treat NPD and its associated symptoms, several considerations are important:

- **Individualized Treatment**: Medication regimens should be tailored to the individual's specific symptoms, co-occurring conditions, and overall health profile. Regular assessment and adjustment of medications are necessary to optimize treatment outcomes.

- **Side Effects and Interactions**: Potential side effects and drug interactions should be carefully monitored. This is particularly important for individuals with NPD, who may have comorbid conditions or be taking multiple medications.
- **Adherence and Compliance**: Ensuring adherence to prescribed medications can be challenging with individuals who have NPD due to their potential mistrust of medical professionals and reluctance to accept treatment. Clear communication and psychoeducation about the benefits and potential side effects of medications can help improve compliance.
- **Combination with Psychotherapy**: Medications are most effective when used in conjunction with psychotherapy. While medications can help manage symptoms, psychotherapy addresses the underlying psychological issues and maladaptive patterns associated with NPD.

Medications can play a supportive role in the treatment of Narcissistic Personality Disorder, particularly in managing co-occurring symptoms such as depression, anxiety, mood swings, and impulsivity. While pharmacotherapy alone is not sufficient to address the core features of NPD, it can enhance the overall effectiveness of treatment when combined with psychotherapy. Individualized treatment plans, careful monitoring, and a holistic approach that includes both medication and therapeutic interventions are essential for achieving the best outcomes for individuals with NPD.

7.3 Challenges in Treating Narcissistic Personality Disorder

Treating Narcissistic Personality Disorder (NPD) presents unique challenges due to the inherent characteristics of the disorder, the complexity of its symptoms, and the interpersonal dynamics involved. This section explores the primary challenges faced by therapists and individuals in the treatment process and offers insights into strategies for overcoming these obstacles.

1. Lack of Insight and Motivation for Change

One of the most significant challenges in treating NPD is the lack of insight and motivation for change among individuals with the disorder. Narcissistic individuals often have an inflated sense of self-importance and a deep-seated belief in their superiority, which can make it difficult for them to recognize the need for therapy or acknowledge their problematic behaviors.

- **Strategies for Overcoming This Challenge**: Building a strong therapeutic alliance is crucial. Therapists need to approach clients with empathy, respect, and non-judgmental acceptance to gradually foster trust. Motivational interviewing techniques can be effective in helping clients explore the discrepancies between their current behaviors and their personal goals, thereby enhancing their motivation for change.

2. Difficulty Establishing a Therapeutic Alliance

NPD is characterized by difficulties in forming and maintaining healthy relationships, including the therapeutic relationship. Individuals with NPD may perceive the therapist as inferior or may attempt to manipulate or dominate the therapy process. They may also be hypersensitive to perceived criticism, which can lead to defensive reactions or withdrawal from therapy.

- **Strategies for Overcoming This Challenge**: Therapists should maintain a balance between validation and confrontation. Providing consistent, genuine empathy while gently challenging maladaptive beliefs and behaviors can help in establishing a stable therapeutic relationship. Setting clear boundaries and expectations from the outset can also help manage potential manipulative behaviors.

3. Resistance to Therapy

Resistance to therapy is common among individuals with NPD. This resistance can manifest in various ways, such as missing appointments, minimizing problems, or rejecting therapeutic interventions. The grandiosity and entitlement associated with NPD can make it difficult for clients to accept feedback or adhere to treatment plans.

- **Strategies for Overcoming This Challenge**: Utilizing a collaborative approach can help reduce resistance. Involving clients in the goal-setting process and allowing them to have a say in their treatment plan can increase their investment in the therapy process. It is also important for therapists to be patient and persistent, acknowledging small steps of progress and continually reinforcing the benefits of therapy.

4. Managing Countertransference

Therapists working with individuals with NPD may experience strong emotional reactions, known as countertransference. These reactions can include feelings of frustration, inadequacy, or anger due to the client's challenging behaviors and attitudes. Managing these emotional responses is essential for maintaining therapeutic effectiveness.

- **Strategies for Overcoming This Challenge**: Regular supervision and peer support can provide therapists with a space to process their feelings and receive guidance. Developing self-awareness and reflective practice can help therapists recognize and manage their countertransference. It's also beneficial to maintain a professional distance and avoid taking clients' behaviors personally.

5. Comorbid Conditions

Individuals with NPD often have comorbid mental health conditions, such as depression, anxiety, substance use disorders, or other personality disorders. These comorbid conditions can complicate the treatment process and require a comprehensive, integrated approach to care.

- **Strategies for Overcoming This Challenge**: A thorough assessment at the outset of treatment can help identify comorbid conditions and inform a more tailored treatment plan. Coordinating care with other healthcare providers, such as psychiatrists or addiction specialists, can ensure a holistic approach to treatment.

Prioritizing the most pressing symptoms and gradually addressing additional issues can enhance overall treatment efficacy.

6. Long-Term Commitment

The treatment of NPD often requires a long-term commitment due to the deeply ingrained nature of narcissistic traits and behaviors. Clients may become impatient with the slow pace of progress or may prematurely terminate therapy once initial symptoms improve.

- **Strategies for Overcoming This Challenge**: Setting realistic expectations at the beginning of therapy is crucial. Helping clients understand that meaningful change takes time and requires ongoing effort can foster a longer-term commitment. Celebrating incremental progress and maintaining a flexible, adaptive treatment plan can keep clients engaged over the long haul.

7. Addressing Underlying Insecurities

Despite their outward appearance of confidence, individuals with NPD often harbor profound insecurities and fears of inadequacy. Addressing these underlying issues can be challenging, as clients may be reluctant to confront their vulnerabilities.

- **Strategies for Overcoming This Challenge**: Gradually introducing exploratory work in a supportive and non-threatening manner can help clients begin to address their insecurities.

Techniques such as psychodynamic therapy, which explores unconscious processes and early experiences, can be particularly effective. Building a safe and trusting therapeutic environment where clients feel comfortable exploring their vulnerabilities is essential.

Treating Narcissistic Personality Disorder is a complex and multifaceted process that requires a nuanced understanding of the disorder, a strong therapeutic alliance, and a comprehensive approach to care. By acknowledging and addressing the unique challenges of treating NPD, therapists can enhance their ability to support individuals in making meaningful and lasting changes. Patience, persistence, and a compassionate approach are key to overcoming these challenges and fostering positive therapeutic outcomes.

7.4 Self-Help Strategies and Support Networks

While professional therapy is crucial in treating Narcissistic Personality Disorder (NPD), self-help strategies and support networks can play a significant role in the recovery and management process. These resources empower individuals with NPD to take an active role in their treatment, providing tools and support that complement formal therapy. This section explores various self-help strategies and the importance of support networks in managing NPD.

Self-Help Strategies

Mindfulness and Meditation

Mindfulness and meditation practices can help individuals with NPD develop greater self-awareness and emotional regulation. By focusing on the present moment and observing thoughts and feelings without judgment, mindfulness can reduce impulsive behaviors and enhance emotional stability.

- Practice: Regular mindfulness meditation sessions, guided mindfulness exercises, and incorporating mindfulness into daily activities can promote long-term benefits.

Journaling

Journaling is a powerful tool for self-reflection and insight. It allows individuals with NPD to explore their thoughts, feelings, and behaviors, helping them identify patterns and triggers.

- Practice: Maintaining a daily journal to record thoughts, emotions, and experiences can provide valuable insights and promote self-understanding.

Setting Realistic Goals

Setting achievable, realistic goals can help individuals with NPD build self-esteem and a sense of accomplishment. It encourages a focus on personal growth and development rather than external validation.

- Practice: Establish short-term and long-term goals that are specific, measurable, attainable, relevant, and time-bound (SMART). Regularly reviewing and adjusting these goals can help maintain motivation and progress.

Developing Empathy

Practicing empathy can help individuals with NPD improve their relationships and reduce self-centered behaviors. Engaging in activities that require understanding and considering others' perspectives can foster empathy.

- Practice: Volunteering, reading literature that explores diverse perspectives, and engaging in active listening exercises can enhance empathy.

Stress Management Techniques

Effective stress management is crucial for emotional regulation and overall well-being. Techniques such as deep breathing, progressive muscle relaxation, and regular physical exercise can reduce stress levels.

- Practice: Incorporate stress management techniques into daily routines to manage anxiety and prevent emotional dysregulation.

Healthy Lifestyle Choices

Maintaining a healthy lifestyle supports mental and physical well-being. Adequate sleep, balanced nutrition, regular physical activity, and avoiding substance abuse are essential components.

- Practice: Establishing routines that promote healthy living can enhance mood, energy levels, and overall resilience.

Support Networks

Family and Friends

Family and friends can provide essential emotional support and encouragement. Educating loved ones about NPD and involving them in the treatment process can foster a supportive environment.

- Practice: Open communication with family and friends, involving them in therapy sessions when appropriate, and seeking their support in managing daily challenges can be beneficial.

Support Groups

Support groups offer a community of individuals who share similar experiences and challenges. These groups provide a safe space to share feelings, receive feedback, and gain different perspectives.

- Practice: Joining a support group specifically tailored for personality disorders or mental health can reduce feelings of isolation and provide valuable peer support.

Online Communities

Online forums and communities can offer support and resources for individuals with NPD. These platforms provide anonymity and access to a wide range of experiences and advice.

- Practice: Participating in reputable online communities and forums dedicated to mental health and NPD can provide additional support and information.

Professional Support Networks

Coordinating care with healthcare providers, including therapists, psychiatrists, and primary care physicians, ensures a comprehensive approach to treatment. These professionals can offer guidance, monitor progress, and adjust treatment plans as needed.

- Practice: Regularly attending therapy sessions, adhering to prescribed treatments, and maintaining open communication with healthcare providers can optimize treatment outcomes.

Educational Resources

Accessing educational resources about NPD can empower individuals to understand their condition better and explore effective coping strategies. Books, articles, and reputable websites can provide valuable information.

- Practice: Reading literature on NPD, attending workshops or webinars, and staying informed about the latest research and treatment approaches can enhance self-awareness and self-management.

Self-help strategies and support networks are vital components in the treatment and management of Narcissistic Personality Disorder. By incorporating mindfulness, journaling, goal-setting, empathy development, stress management, and healthy lifestyle choices into daily routines, individuals with NPD can actively contribute to their recovery. Additionally, leveraging the support of family, friends, support groups, online communities, professional networks, and educational resources provides a comprehensive framework for managing NPD. These combined efforts can lead to improved self-awareness, emotional regulation, and interpersonal relationships, ultimately fostering a more balanced and fulfilling life.

Chapter 8: Moving Forward: Healing and Growth

The journey toward healing and growth for individuals with Narcissistic Personality Disorder (NPD) is both challenging and rewarding. This chapter delves into the process of moving forward after diagnosis and initial treatment, highlighting the paths to personal development, improved relationships, and sustained mental health. It focuses on the steps individuals can take to maintain progress, build resilience, and create a fulfilling life beyond the constraints of their disorder.

Embracing Self-Awareness

Self-awareness is a critical component of healing for those with NPD. It involves recognizing and understanding one's thoughts, emotions, and behaviors and their impact on oneself and others. Developing self-awareness can be a gradual process, facilitated by continuous self-reflection, mindfulness practices, and ongoing therapy. As individuals gain deeper insights into their narcissistic patterns, they become better equipped to manage their impulses and make more conscious choices.

Fostering Genuine Relationships

Healthy relationships are integral to emotional well-being and personal growth. For individuals with NPD, fostering genuine relationships requires a shift from seeking admiration and validation to building mutual respect and empathy. This transformation involves active listening, expressing vulnerability, and valuing the needs and feelings of others. Over time, these efforts can lead to more meaningful connections and a support system that reinforces positive behaviors and attitudes.

Commitment to Continuous Learning

Personal growth is an ongoing journey that extends beyond initial therapy. Individuals with NPD benefit from a lifelong commitment to learning and self-improvement. This can include reading self-help books, attending workshops, and engaging in educational programs focused on emotional intelligence, communication skills, and conflict resolution. Continuous learning helps individuals stay adaptable and open to new perspectives, which is crucial for sustained growth.

Developing Resilience

Resilience is the ability to cope with adversity and bounce back from challenges. For individuals with NPD, developing resilience involves building coping strategies to manage stress, setbacks, and emotional triggers. This can be achieved through regular practice of stress management techniques, such as deep breathing, exercise, and mindfulness. Additionally, fostering a positive mindset and cultivating gratitude can enhance resilience and overall mental health.

Setting and Achieving Personal Goals

Goal-setting is a powerful tool for fostering growth and motivation. Setting realistic and meaningful goals provides individuals with a sense of purpose and direction. These goals should be specific, measurable, attainable, relevant, and time-bound (SMART). Regularly reviewing and adjusting goals helps maintain focus and motivation, ensuring continuous progress. Celebrating achievements, no matter how small, reinforces positive behaviors and encourages further growth.

Practicing Self-Compassion

Self-compassion is essential for healing from NPD. It involves treating oneself with kindness and understanding, especially in moments of failure or difficulty. Practicing self-compassion reduces the harsh self-criticism often associated with narcissistic tendencies and promotes emotional healing. Techniques such as self-soothing, positive self-talk, and mindfulness can cultivate a compassionate attitude toward oneself.

Engaging in Meaningful Activities

Engaging in activities that bring joy and fulfillment contributes significantly to overall well-being. Individuals with NPD should explore hobbies, volunteer work, and creative pursuits that align with their interests and values. These activities provide a sense of accomplishment and satisfaction that is not dependent on external validation. They also offer opportunities to connect with others who share similar passions, fostering a sense of community and belonging.

Maintaining a Balanced Lifestyle

A balanced lifestyle supports sustained mental health and personal growth. This includes maintaining a healthy diet, getting regular exercise, ensuring adequate sleep, and avoiding substance abuse. A balanced lifestyle also involves managing work-life balance, setting boundaries, and taking time for relaxation and self-care. Prioritizing physical and mental health creates a stable foundation for ongoing personal development.

Seeking Support When Needed

The journey of healing and growth is not without its challenges. There will be times when individuals with NPD need additional support. Continuing therapy, whether regularly or as needed, provides a valuable resource for navigating difficulties and maintaining progress. Support groups, both in-person and online, offer a community of individuals with shared experiences who can provide encouragement and advice.

Moving forward from Narcissistic Personality Disorder is a multifaceted process that requires dedication, self-reflection, and a commitment to personal growth. By embracing self-awareness, fostering genuine relationships, committing to continuous learning, developing resilience, setting and achieving goals, practicing self-compassion, engaging in meaningful activities, maintaining a balanced lifestyle, and seeking support when needed, individuals with NPD can create a more fulfilling and balanced life. The path to healing and growth is a lifelong journey, but with perseverance and support, it is a journey that leads to profound transformation and well-being.

8.1 Building Healthy Relationships Post-Narcissism

Building healthy relationships post-narcissism involves a fundamental shift in how individuals with Narcissistic Personality Disorder (NPD) interact with others. This process requires addressing ingrained patterns of behavior, developing empathy, and learning to value mutual respect and genuine connection over superficial admiration and control. The following sections outline key strategies and steps for fostering healthy, sustainable relationships after addressing narcissistic tendencies.

Embracing Vulnerability

One of the core challenges for individuals with NPD is the fear of vulnerability. Narcissistic traits often develop as a defense mechanism against deep-seated insecurities and fears of inadequacy. To build healthy relationships, it's essential to embrace vulnerability. This means being open and honest about one's feelings, needs, and experiences without fear of judgment or rejection. By allowing themselves to be vulnerable, individuals with NPD can create deeper, more authentic connections with others.

Developing Empathy

Empathy is the ability to understand and share the feelings of others. For individuals with NPD, developing empathy can be particularly challenging but is crucial for building healthy relationships. Empathy involves actively listening to others, acknowledging their emotions, and responding with compassion. Practicing empathy can help individuals with NPD shift their focus from self-centered concerns to a more balanced perspective that values the experiences and feelings of others.

Practicing Active Listening

Active listening is a vital skill for effective communication and relationship building. It involves fully concentrating on what the other person is saying, without interrupting or immediately forming a response. Active listening requires paying attention to both verbal and non-verbal cues, such as body language and tone of voice. By practicing active listening, individuals with NPD can show genuine interest in others and foster a sense of mutual respect and understanding.

Setting and Respecting Boundaries

Healthy relationships are built on the foundation of clear and respectful boundaries. For individuals with NPD, understanding and respecting boundaries can be challenging due to tendencies toward control and entitlement. Learning to set personal boundaries and respect the boundaries of others is essential. This includes recognizing when to give others space, avoiding intrusive behaviors, and being mindful of how one's actions affect others. Establishing and maintaining healthy boundaries helps create a safe and respectful relational environment.

Fostering Mutual Respect

Mutual respect is a cornerstone of any healthy relationship. It involves valuing others as equals and treating them with consideration and dignity. For individuals with NPD, fostering mutual respect requires a shift from viewing relationships as hierarchical to recognizing the inherent worth of others. This involves acknowledging the contributions, feelings, and perspectives of others and refraining from behaviors that undermine their self-esteem or autonomy.

Cultivating Patience and Understanding

Building healthy relationships takes time and effort. It requires patience and a willingness to understand that change is a gradual process. Individuals with NPD need to be patient with themselves and others as they navigate the complexities of new relational dynamics. This includes being forgiving of mistakes, understanding that setbacks are part of growth, and continually striving to improve communication and relational skills.

Engaging in Shared Activities

Shared activities provide opportunities to bond and build connections based on common interests and experiences. Engaging in activities together, whether it's a hobby, sport, or volunteer work, can strengthen relationships by fostering collaboration and mutual enjoyment. Shared activities also create positive experiences that can help offset past negative interactions and build a foundation of trust and goodwill.

Seeking Feedback and Reflecting on Interactions

Seeking feedback from trusted individuals and reflecting on interactions can provide valuable insights into one's behavior and its impact on others. Constructive feedback helps individuals with NPD identify areas for improvement and develop more adaptive relational strategies. Reflecting on interactions allows for a deeper understanding of relational patterns and the opportunity to make conscious adjustments to foster healthier connections.

Prioritizing Emotional Health

Emotional health is critical for maintaining healthy relationships. This involves managing stress, regulating emotions, and seeking support when needed. Practices such as mindfulness, meditation, and regular self-care can enhance emotional well-being. Additionally, continuing therapy or counseling can provide ongoing support and guidance in navigating relational challenges and maintaining progress.

Building healthy relationships post-narcissism is a transformative journey that requires commitment, self-awareness, and a willingness to change. By embracing vulnerability, developing empathy, practicing active listening, setting and respecting boundaries, fostering mutual respect, cultivating patience, engaging in shared activities, seeking feedback, and prioritizing emotional health, individuals with NPD can create meaningful and lasting connections. The path to healthier relationships is an integral part of the broader journey toward healing and personal growth, leading to a more fulfilling and balanced life.

8.2 Personal Growth and Self-Reflection

Personal growth and self-reflection are pivotal for individuals recovering from Narcissistic Personality Disorder (NPD). This journey involves a continuous process of self-examination, learning, and transformation. It requires acknowledging past behaviors, understanding their origins, and actively working towards positive change. This chapter explores strategies for fostering personal growth and the importance of self-reflection in achieving a healthier, more balanced self-identity.

Embracing Self-Awareness

Self-awareness is the foundation of personal growth. It involves recognizing one's thoughts, feelings, and behaviors and understanding how they impact oneself and others. For individuals with NPD, developing self-awareness can be challenging due to tendencies toward denial and self-deception. However, through consistent practice and support, it is possible to cultivate a deeper understanding of oneself. Techniques such as mindfulness meditation, journaling, and regular therapy sessions can enhance self-awareness, providing insights into narcissistic patterns and triggers.

Practicing Honest Self-Reflection

Honest self-reflection is crucial for personal growth. It requires individuals to critically examine their actions, motivations, and the consequences of their behavior. This process involves acknowledging past mistakes and understanding the underlying reasons for narcissistic tendencies. By reflecting honestly, individuals with NPD can identify areas for improvement and develop a more realistic and balanced self-concept. Self-reflection can be facilitated through regular journaling, where individuals document their thoughts and experiences, and by seeking feedback from trusted friends, family members, or therapists.

Setting Personal Goals

Setting personal goals is a powerful tool for fostering growth and motivation. Goals provide direction and a sense of purpose, helping individuals focus their efforts on meaningful change. For individuals with NPD, it is essential to set realistic and achievable goals that align with their values and long-term aspirations. These goals should be specific, measurable, attainable, relevant, and time-bound (SMART). By regularly reviewing and adjusting their goals, individuals can maintain motivation and track their progress. Celebrating small achievements along the way reinforces positive behaviors and encourages continued growth.

Developing Emotional Intelligence

Emotional intelligence (EI) involves understanding and managing one's emotions and recognizing and influencing the emotions of others. High EI is associated with better relationships, effective communication, and overall well-being. For individuals with NPD, developing emotional intelligence can help mitigate narcissistic tendencies and improve interpersonal interactions. Techniques such as empathy training, active listening exercises, and emotional regulation strategies can enhance EI.

Additionally, therapy can provide a structured environment for developing and practicing these skills.

Cultivating Empathy

Empathy is the ability to understand and share the feelings of others. It is a critical component of healthy relationships and personal growth. For individuals with NPD, cultivating empathy involves shifting focus from oneself to others and genuinely caring about their experiences and emotions. Empathy can be developed through practices such as perspective-taking, where individuals consciously consider others' viewpoints, and by engaging in activities that promote compassionate behavior, such as volunteering or community service.

Managing Stress and Practicing Self-Care

Managing stress and practicing self-care are essential for maintaining emotional and physical well-being. Chronic stress can exacerbate narcissistic tendencies and hinder personal growth. Techniques such as deep breathing, progressive muscle relaxation, and regular physical exercise can help manage stress levels. Additionally, engaging in self-care activities that promote relaxation and enjoyment, such as hobbies, spending time in nature, or practicing mindfulness, can enhance overall well-being and resilience.

Seeking Continuous Learning and Growth

Personal growth is a lifelong journey that involves continuous learning and development. Individuals with NPD can benefit from exploring new interests, acquiring new skills, and expanding their knowledge. This can include attending workshops, enrolling in courses, reading self-help books, and seeking out educational resources that promote emotional and psychological well-being. Continuous learning keeps individuals adaptable and open to new perspectives, fostering ongoing personal development.

Building a Supportive Network

A supportive network of friends, family, and professionals is invaluable for personal growth. Trusted individuals can provide encouragement, feedback, and accountability, helping individuals with NPD stay on track with their goals. Support groups, both in-person and online, offer a sense of community and shared experience, reducing feelings of isolation. Regular therapy sessions with a qualified mental health professional can provide structured support and guidance throughout the personal growth journey.

Celebrating Progress and Milestones

Celebrating progress and milestones is important for maintaining motivation and reinforcing positive change. Acknowledging achievements, no matter how small, helps individuals recognize their efforts and stay committed to their growth journey. Celebrations can take various forms, from personal reflections and journaling to sharing successes with supportive friends or family members. Recognizing progress fosters a sense of accomplishment and encourages continued efforts toward self-improvement.

Personal growth and self-reflection are integral components of the recovery journey for individuals with Narcissistic Personality Disorder. By embracing self-awareness, practicing honest self-reflection, setting personal goals, developing emotional intelligence, cultivating empathy, managing stress, seeking continuous learning, building a supportive network, and celebrating progress, individuals can achieve significant transformation. This journey is a lifelong commitment to self-improvement and emotional well-being, leading to a more balanced and fulfilling life.

8.3 Raising Awareness and Reducing Stigma

Raising awareness and reducing the stigma surrounding Narcissistic Personality Disorder (NPD) is crucial for fostering understanding, empathy, and effective treatment. Misconceptions and negative stereotypes about NPD can create barriers to seeking help and support, both for individuals with the disorder and their loved ones. This chapter explores strategies for increasing public awareness, promoting accurate information, and reducing the stigma associated with NPD.

Educating the Public

Public education is fundamental in raising awareness about NPD. Many people have misconceptions about what NPD entails, often viewing it solely through a lens of selfishness and arrogance without understanding the underlying psychological complexities. Educational campaigns can provide accurate information about the symptoms, causes, and treatment options for NPD. These campaigns can be conducted through various media, including social media platforms, websites, public service announcements, and community workshops. By presenting factual information, these initiatives can help demystify NPD and promote a more nuanced understanding of the disorder.

Sharing Personal Stories

Personal stories can be powerful tools for reducing stigma and fostering empathy. When individuals with NPD or their loved ones share their experiences, it humanizes the disorder and highlights the challenges and triumphs associated with it. Personal narratives can be shared through blogs, podcasts, video series, or public speaking engagements. These stories not only provide hope and encouragement to others facing similar challenges but also educate the broader public about the realities of living with NPD.

Promoting Empathy and Compassion

Encouraging empathy and compassion towards individuals with NPD is essential for reducing stigma. Empathy involves understanding and sharing the feelings of others, while compassion involves a willingness to help. Promoting these values can be achieved through educational programs that focus on emotional intelligence and the importance of understanding mental health issues. Schools, workplaces, and community organizations can implement programs that teach empathy and compassion, helping to create a more supportive and inclusive environment for those with NPD.

Engaging Healthcare Providers

Healthcare providers play a critical role in raising awareness and reducing stigma. By receiving training on NPD and other personality disorders, healthcare professionals can provide more accurate diagnoses, effective treatments, and compassionate care. Continuing education programs for mental health professionals, primary care physicians, and other healthcare workers can ensure that they are equipped with the latest knowledge and best practices for managing NPD. Additionally, healthcare providers can advocate for their patients and work to reduce stigma within the medical community.

Supporting Research and Advocacy

Supporting research into the causes, treatment, and management of NPD is vital for advancing our understanding of the disorder and improving outcomes for those affected. Advocacy for increased funding and resources for NPD research can lead to better diagnostic tools, more effective therapies, and a greater overall understanding of the disorder. Organizations dedicated to mental health advocacy can play a pivotal role in lobbying for research funding and promoting policies that support individuals with NPD and their families.

Creating Supportive Communities

Building supportive communities where individuals with NPD and their loved ones can find understanding and acceptance is crucial for reducing stigma. Support groups, both in-person and online, provide safe spaces for sharing experiences, seeking advice, and offering mutual support. Community organizations can also host events and workshops that focus on mental health awareness and support, fostering a sense of belonging and reducing feelings of isolation.

Addressing Media Representations

Media representations of NPD often perpetuate stereotypes and misinformation. By addressing and challenging these portrayals, we can promote a more accurate and compassionate understanding of the disorder. Media literacy programs can teach individuals to critically evaluate how mental health issues are depicted in the media and to seek out reliable sources of information. Engaging with media creators to encourage more nuanced and respectful portrayals of NPD can also help shift public perceptions.

Encouraging Open Dialogue

Creating an environment where open dialogue about NPD is encouraged can help reduce stigma and promote understanding. This involves fostering conversations about mental health in various settings, such as schools, workplaces, and community centers. Encouraging people to speak openly about their experiences with NPD and other mental health issues can help normalize these conversations and reduce the shame and stigma often associated with them.

Providing Resources and Support

Access to resources and support is essential for individuals with NPD and their families. Providing information about local mental health services, support groups, and educational materials can empower individuals to seek help and support. Community organizations, healthcare providers, and mental health advocates can collaborate to ensure that these resources are widely available and easily accessible.

Raising awareness and reducing the stigma surrounding Narcissistic Personality Disorder is a multifaceted effort that involves education, empathy, and advocacy. By educating the public, sharing personal stories, promoting empathy and compassion, engaging healthcare providers, supporting research, creating supportive communities, addressing media representations, encouraging open dialogue, and providing resources and support, we can foster a more understanding and inclusive society. These efforts not only benefit individuals with NPD but also contribute to the overall mental health and well-being of the community.

8.4 Future Directions in Research and Treatment

The future of research and treatment for Narcissistic Personality Disorder (NPD) holds promise for more effective interventions, a deeper understanding of the disorder's underlying mechanisms, and improved outcomes for those affected. This chapter explores emerging trends and future directions in the field, emphasizing the importance of continued innovation and collaboration in advancing the science and practice of treating NPD.

Advancements in Neurobiological Research

One of the most promising areas of future research involves the neurobiological underpinnings of NPD. Advances in neuroimaging techniques, such as functional magnetic resonance imaging (fMRI) and positron emission tomography (PET), are providing new insights into the brain structures and functions associated with narcissistic traits. Understanding the neural correlates of empathy, self-regulation, and emotional processing in individuals with NPD can inform the development of targeted treatments. Future research may uncover specific biomarkers that can aid in the early diagnosis and differentiation of NPD from other personality disorders.

Genetic Studies

Genetic research is another critical avenue for understanding NPD. Studies investigating the heritability of narcissistic traits and the identification of genetic variants associated with the disorder can shed light on its biological foundations. As genetic technologies advance, large-scale genome-wide association studies (GWAS) may identify genetic markers that contribute to the development of NPD. These discoveries could lead to personalized treatment approaches based on an individual's genetic profile, enhancing the efficacy of interventions.

Psychotherapy Innovations

Psychotherapy remains a cornerstone of NPD treatment, and future directions involve refining existing therapeutic approaches and developing new ones. Integrative therapies that combine elements of cognitive-behavioral therapy (CBT), psychodynamic therapy, and dialectical behavior therapy (DBT) show promise. Innovations such as schema therapy, which focuses on identifying and altering maladaptive schemas developed in childhood, offer potential benefits for individuals with NPD. Future research should continue to evaluate the effectiveness of these integrative approaches and explore how they can be tailored to the unique needs of individuals with NPD.

Technology-Enhanced Interventions

The integration of technology into mental health treatment is an emerging trend with significant implications for NPD. Digital platforms, mobile applications, and virtual reality (VR) therapies can provide accessible and scalable interventions. These technologies can offer self-monitoring tools, psychoeducation, and therapeutic exercises that individuals can use outside traditional therapy sessions. Virtual reality, in particular, holds the potential for immersive experiences that help individuals with NPD develop empathy and practice social skills in a controlled environment. Future research should focus on the development, validation, and implementation of technology-enhanced interventions for NPD.

Pharmacological Treatments

While psychotherapy is the primary treatment for NPD, pharmacological approaches may also play a role in managing certain symptoms. Research into the neurochemical imbalances associated with NPD could lead to the development of medications that target specific pathways involved in emotional regulation, impulsivity, and aggression. Clinical trials investigating the efficacy and safety of these medications will be crucial. Additionally, combination treatments that integrate pharmacotherapy with psychotherapy may enhance overall treatment outcomes.

Early Intervention and Prevention

Early intervention and prevention strategies are vital for reducing the prevalence and impact of NPD. Identifying at-risk individuals, such as children and adolescents exhibiting early signs of narcissistic traits, can facilitate timely intervention. Educational programs for parents, teachers, and healthcare providers can promote awareness and early detection. Preventive interventions that focus on fostering healthy self-esteem, empathy, and emotional regulation in young people can mitigate the development of narcissistic traits. Longitudinal studies tracking the effectiveness of these early interventions will provide valuable data for refining prevention strategies.

Cultural and Contextual Considerations

Understanding the cultural and contextual factors that influence the expression and treatment of NPD is essential for developing culturally sensitive interventions. Future research should explore how cultural norms, values, and societal changes impact the manifestation of narcissistic traits and the acceptance of treatment. Cross-cultural studies can identify universal aspects of NPD as well as culturally specific manifestations and challenges. This knowledge can inform the adaptation of therapeutic approaches to better meet the needs of diverse populations.

Collaborative and Multidisciplinary Approaches

Advancing the field of NPD research and treatment requires collaboration across disciplines, including psychology, psychiatry, neuroscience, genetics, and social work. Multidisciplinary teams can integrate diverse perspectives and expertise to develop comprehensive and effective interventions. Collaborative research networks and consortia can facilitate large-scale studies, data sharing, and the dissemination of findings. Engaging stakeholders, including individuals with NPD, their families, and advocacy groups, in the research process, can ensure that the development of treatments is patient-centered and responsive to the needs of those affected.

The future of NPD research and treatment is marked by exciting opportunities for innovation and advancement. By embracing new technologies, refining therapeutic approaches, exploring genetic and neurobiological underpinnings, and fostering early intervention and prevention, the field can move towards more effective and personalized treatments. Collaborative efforts and a commitment to cultural sensitivity will further enhance our ability to support individuals with NPD in achieving meaningful recovery and improved quality of life.

Conclusion

"The Psychology of Narcissism: Understanding Narcissistic Personality Disorder and its Impact on Relationships, Work, and Self-Identity" delves deep into the intricate complexities of Narcissistic Personality Disorder (NPD) and its profound effects on individuals and their environments. Throughout this journey, we have explored the multifaceted nature of NPD, from its historical roots and theoretical underpinnings to its manifestation in various contexts such as relationships, workplaces, and personal identity.

Narcissism, characterized by a pervasive pattern of grandiosity, a need for admiration, and a lack of empathy, presents significant challenges for both those who live with it and those who interact with it. We have examined the diagnostic criteria, distinguishing NPD from other personality disorders, and delved into the nuanced subtypes of grandiose and vulnerable narcissism, each presenting unique challenges and dynamics.

In understanding the developmental factors, genetic influences, and environmental contributors to NPD, we have gained insights into how early experiences and parenting styles shape narcissistic traits. These insights are crucial for developing effective therapeutic interventions and prevention strategies.

The impact of narcissism on relationships, whether romantic partnerships or parenting dynamics, highlights the detrimental effects on emotional intimacy, trust, and mutual respect. In the workplace, narcissistic leadership can influence organizational culture and productivity, posing challenges that require strategic management and intervention.

Exploring self-identity within the context of narcissism reveals the intricate interplay between self-esteem, external validation, and the pursuit of perfection. We have discussed strategies for personal growth, self-reflection, and building healthy relationships post-narcissism, emphasizing empathy, vulnerability, and mutual respect as essential components of healing.

Treatment approaches, including psychotherapy, medications, and self-help strategies, offer hope for individuals seeking to manage symptoms and improve their quality of life. Challenges in treatment underscore the need for tailored interventions that address the unique needs and complexities of NPD.

Looking forward, the future of NPD research and treatment holds promise for advancements in neurobiological understanding, innovative therapies, and early intervention strategies. By raising awareness, reducing stigma, and promoting empathy, we can create a more supportive and inclusive environment for individuals living with NPD and their families.

"The Psychology of Narcissism" invites readers to deepen their understanding of this complex disorder, fostering empathy and compassion while advocating for effective treatment and support. By integrating knowledge, research, and lived experiences, we can strive towards a future where individuals with Narcissistic Personality Disorder find hope, healing, and empowerment in their journey toward wellness and self-discovery.